ROAD

Brunton Terrace

Maryfield

Maryfield Place

Lady Menzies Place

Regent Place

Waverl

LON

D0007148

Easter Road

MONTROSE TERRACE

Jime Street

Abbey

Street

Abbey

Street

ABBEYHILL

Stanley Place

Regent Terrace Mews

Terrace

ROAD

Abbeymount

Abbeyhill

Croft-An-Righ

Tytler Gardens

Milton

Street

Waverley Park

Spring

Gardens

Clockmill

Lane

Royal Park Terrace

MEADOWBANK

Crescent

Abbeyhill

Abbeyhill

Horse Wynd

Palace of
Holyroodhouse

Holyrood
Abbey

Scottish
Parliament
Building

Queen's Drive

Queen's

Drive

St Margaret's
Loch

Our
Dynamic
Earth

P

Holyrood Park

Salisbury
Crags

251

Arthur's
Seat

Bank

Queen's

Drive

H

J

K

# CITYPACK TOP 25
# Edinburgh

**HILARY WESTON AND JACKIE STADDON**

If you have any comments
or suggestions for this guide
you can contact the editor at
*Citypack@theAA.com*

**AA Publishing**
Find out more about AA Publishing and the wide
range of services the AA provides by visiting our
website at www.theAA.com/travel

# How to Use This Book

## KEY TO SYMBOLS

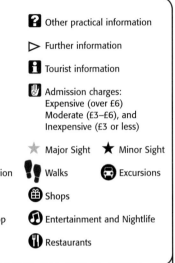

| | | | |
|---|---|---|---|
| ✚ | Map reference to the accompanying fold-out map | 🅿 | Other practical information |
| ✉ | Address | ▷ | Further information |
| ☎ | Telephone number | ℹ | Tourist information |
| 🕓 | Opening/closing times | ✋ | Admission charges: Expensive (over £6) Moderate (£3–£6), and Inexpensive (£3 or less) |
| 🍴 | Restaurant or café | | |
| 🚆 | Nearest rail station | ★ Major Sight   ★ Minor Sight |
| Ⓜ | Nearest subway (Metro) station | 👣 Walks   🚌 Excursions |
| 🚍 | Nearest bus route | 🎪 Shops |
| ⛴ | Nearest riverboat or ferry stop | 🎵 Entertainment and Nightlife |
| ♿ | Facilities for visitors with disabilities | 🍽 Restaurants |

### This guide is divided into four sections

• **Essential Edinburgh:** an introduction to the city and tips on making the most of your stay.

• **Edinburgh by Area:** We've broken the city into four areas, and recommended the best sights, shops, entertainment venues, nightlife and restaurants in each one. Suggested walks help you to explore on foot.

• **Where to Stay:** the best hotels, whether you're looking for luxury, budget or something in between.

• **Need to Know:** the info you need to make your trip run smoothly, including getting about by public transport, weather tips, emergency phone numbers and useful websites.

**Navigation** In the Edinburgh by Area chapter, we've given each area its own tint, which is also used on the locator maps throughout the book and the map on the inside front cover.

**Maps** The fold-out map accompanying this book is a comprehensive street plan of Edinburgh. The grid on this fold-out map is the same as the grid on the locator maps within the book. We've given grid references within the book for each sight and listing.

# Contents

# Introducing Edinburgh

Edinburgh, the striking capital of Scotland, attracts many thousands of visitors every year. They come for many reasons: to seek their ancestral roots, to experience the Festival or just to get a taste of what makes Scotland tick.

Whatever the reason for the visit, few first-time visitors are prepared for the sheer majesty of the city and the richness of its history and culture. Edinburgh effortlessly combines its past with all that's best in 21st-century life, making it a popular, year-round destination and a jumping-off point for exploring the rest of Scotland.

Reminders of the past are everywhere in Edinburgh. The castle rises majestically over the tall tenements, narrow streets and dark *vennels* (alleyways) of the Old Town, while, to the north, the broad streets and spacious squares of the New Town are lined with gracious 18th-century buildings. Look closer, though, and it becomes clear that the city is no time warp, a tourist hub existing as a living museum or theme park of the Enlightenment. Scotland's official capital since 1532, Edinburgh today is home to the country's devolved government, whose parliament building, regardless of the final cost, is the public face of surging national confidence. Devolved regional government has created hundreds of jobs. The economy is dominated by the service sector, with the emphasis on financial services, which has encouraged growing numbers of young, ambitious, highly paid professionals. It's these people, rather than the numerous visitors, who have truly charged the city's renaissance, turning the capital into a slick and stylish metropolis, whose quality of life is rated among the highest in the UK.

Take time to participate in some of the pleasures enjoyed by local people—plays, music, bar-hopping and the club scene—rather than a steady diet of tartan-obsessed Caledonian entertainment.

## Facts + Figures

- The population of Edinburgh is around half a million.
- The New Town contains more than 3,000 listed buildings.
- The highest point is Arthur's Seat.

### PRINCES STREET

Princes Street, despite its World Heritage status, has long been an architectural blot, a string of tasteless identical buildings housing chain stores. Hope is at hand, with plans to demolish some of the worst buildings and replace them with quality shopping malls and expensive housing, a scheme due for completion by 2015.

## MILITARY TATTOO

You'll need to book early for this one. The spectacle, held on the castle Esplanade with military precision–the swirl of the kilts, the sound of the pipes–is the greatest tattoo of them all. Tickets: ☎ 0870 555 118, www.edintattoo.co.uk (on sale from early Mar). Takes place for three weeks in August.

## FESTIVAL TIME

Edinburgh's Festival is not one event but many, running concurrently in August. The most prestigious is the Edinburgh International Festival, founded in 1947, which showcases world-class performing arts events. Side by side with this heavyweight, the anarchic and vast Fringe has plays, music, comedy and dance in nearly 300 venues.

# A Short Stay in Edinburgh

**DAY 1**

**Morning** Most popular is a stroll down the **Royal Mile** (▷ 28–29). Those who don't want to walk can take the **hop-on-hop-off bus** (▷ 119) to visit the major sights. Get to **Edinburgh Castle** (▷ 24–25) at opening time to avoid the crowds. Close by is the **Tartan Weaving Mill** (▷ 35) and the **Camera Obscura** (▷ 32). Take a bit of time to explore the alleyways (*vennels* and *wynds*) as you go away from the castle along Castlehill.

**Mid-morning** Take a look on the right at Victoria Street, with its specialist shops. If you want to walk farther, continue onto West Bow and out into the attractive **Grassmarket** (▷ 32–33), with lots of opportunities for coffee. Retrace your steps and continue along the Royal Mile into Lawnmarket and along to High Street. Take a look at **St. Giles' Cathedral** (▷ 30).

**Lunch** Just past the cathedral, have lunch at **Wee Windaes** (▷ 44).

**Afternoon** Continue on High Street, where you will find the **Museum of Childhood** (▷ 54–55) and **John Knox House** (▷ 60) opposite. Continue onto Canongate, with the **Museum of Edinburgh** (▷ 53) on the right and **Canongate Tolbooth** (▷ 50–51) on the left. As you near the end of the road you will see the dramatic **Scottish Parliament Building** (▷ 57) on the right and shortly afterward the **Palace of Holyroodhouse** (▷ 58–59).

**Dinner** For old-fashioned charm at a price try the **Witchery by the Castle** (▷ 44). For more modern dining, check out **Shaws Bistro and International Tapas Bar** (▷ 44).

**Evening** Just to the west of the Old Town you will find **Usher Hall** (▷ 41), where you can take in a classical concert. If clubbing is more your thing try the **Liquid Room** (▷ 41) for cutting-edge sounds.

ESSENTIAL EDINBURGH  A SHORT STAY IN EDINBURGH

## DAY 2

**Morning** Start at the Waverley Station end of **Princes Street** (▷ 74). You can then decide if you want to explore the shops along the famous road or those behind it. Those preferring art can visit the **National Gallery of Scotland** (▷ 70–71), just beyond the **Scott Monument** (▷ 76). It is possible to take the free link bus from here to the other galleries.

**Mid-morning** Have a coffee at the gallery or try the **Forth Floor Restaurant** (▷ 84, panel) at Harvey Nichols on **Multrees Walk** (▷ 79, panel), just to the north of Princes Street. You can then explore the other designer shops on The Walk.

**Lunch** Take a pub lunch on Rose Street, which once boasted the most pubs of any street in Edinburgh. The **Mussel Inn** (▷ 86) is a good choice for seafood lovers.

**Afternoon** Catch a bus from Princes Street out to **Leith** (▷ 94–95) and visit the **Royal Yacht** *Britannia* (▷ 97) and the **Ocean Terminal Centre** (▷ 104). Take a walk along The Shore, with its trendy bars and smart restaurants.

**Dinner** Back in New Town, eat on the popular George Street. Try the Italian **Est Est Est** (▷ 84) or for smart dining, the **Dome** (▷ 84).

**Evening** Still on George Street, try the most fashionable clubs **Lulu** (▷ 83) or **Shanghai** (▷ 83) in the boutique hotels Tigerlily and Le Monde. Try the Omni Centre at Greenside Place on Leith Street for cinema or a comedy show, or the **Edinburgh Playhouse** (▷ 82) for musicals, dance or rock concerts. If you want some home-grown fun, try the dinner show **Jamie's Scottish Evening** (▷ 82) at the Thistle Hotel.

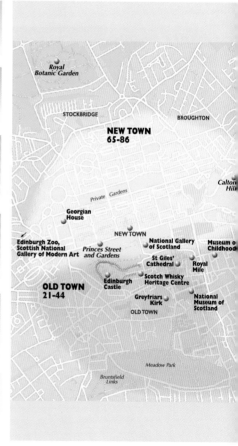
ESSENTIAL EDINBURGH  TOP 25

►►►

**Arthur's Seat ▷ 48–49**
Looming above the city, this hill, an extinct volcano, is some 325 million years old.

**Calton Hill ▷ 68** Known as the Athens of the North in the 18th century—its buildings tell you why.

**Canongate Tolbooth ▷ 50–51** This attractive building houses a museum of everyday life.

**Scottish Parliament Building ▷ 57** Controversial, expensive, but certainly striking.

**Scottish National Gallery of Modern Art ▷ 98** The place to view 20th-century Scottish art and sculpture.

**Scotch Whisky Heritage Centre ▷ 31** Your chance to taste a wee dram of Scotland's national drink.

**St. Giles' Cathedral ▷ 30** The imposing church dedicated to the patron saint of the city.

**Royal Yacht *Britannia* ▷ 97** All aboard the most famous of ships—a must for royal buffs.

**Royal Mile ▷ 28–29** The straight road all the way from Edinburgh Castle to Palace of Holyroodhouse.

**Royal Botanic Garden ▷ 96** A green oasis in a busy capital—there's year-round interest here.

**Princes Street and Gardens ▷ 74** After shopping in this famous street, relax in the gardens.

**Palace of Holyroodhouse ▷ 58–59** A royal palace rich with historical associations and works of art.

8

These pages are a quick guide to the Top 25, which are described in more detail later. Here they are listed alphabetically, and the tinted background shows which area they are in.

**Craigmillar Castle**
▷ **90–91** A trip out to this castle makes a pleasant change from city bustle.

**Edinburgh Castle**
▷ **24–25** One million visitors a year come to view Scotland's oldest castle.

**Edinburgh Zoo** ▷ **92–93**
A conscientious approach to showing animals and their conservation.

**Georgian House** ▷ **69**
The epitome of 18th-century New Town elegance is well worth a visit.

**Greyfriars Kirk** ▷ **26**
Lots of elaborate memorials and the most famous of all, Greyfriars Bobby.

**Holyrood Park** ▷ **52**
Take a walk on the wild side in this pleasant park.

**Leith** ▷ **94–95**
Edinburgh's seaport and now a trendy tourist area.

**Museum of Childhood**
▷ **54–55** Nostalgia and fun in this museum for big and little kids.

**Museum of Edinburgh**
▷ **53** A treasure house of information and objects all about Edinburgh.

**National Gallery of Scotland** ▷ **70–71** A breathtaking collection of artistic masterpieces.

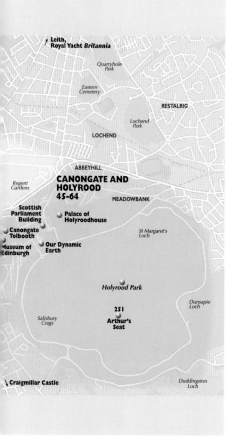

Leith,
Royal Yacht *Britannia*
Quarryhole Park
Eastern Cemetery
RESTALRIG
Lochend Park
LOCHEND
ABBEYHILL
Regent Gardens
CANONGATE AND HOLYROOD 45-64
MEADOWBANK
Scottish Parliament Building
Palace of Holyroodhouse
Canongate Tolbooth
St Margaret's Loch
Museum of Edinburgh
Our Dynamic Earth
Holyrood Park
Dunsapie Loch
Salisbury Crags
251
Arthur's Seat
Craigmillar Castle
Duddingston Loch

**Our Dynamic Earth**
▷ **56** Fun science with great effects and interactive enjoyment.

**New Town** ▷ **72–73**
18th-century planning at its best—a prime example of Georgian architecture.

**National Museum of Scotland** ▷ **27** An entertaining introduction to Scottish history and culture.

◀ ◀ ◀

# Shopping

Once overshadowed by the glitz of the city of Glasgow, Edinburgh has now won serious shoppers from all over Scotland, as well as countless visitors. Explore by foot to find the best of Scotland on offer.

### Get Off the Beaten Track
Shops on Princes Street may be little more than a string of high-street names, and malls ring the suburbs, but away from these Edinburgh offers some of the best shopping in Europe. International names contrast with specialist outlets offering the best of Scottish products, and the goods and service of traditional retailers are hard to find elsewhere. These temples to commerce are housed in a wonderful variety of buildings, ranging from stolid Victorian respectability and glass-and-steel modernity to idiosyncratic individual shops with a quirky charm all their own. The tip is to get off the main drags, away from the crowds, and onto the side streets and alleyways to see everything from custom-made bagpipes to cashmere as soft as a cloud.

### Made in Scotland
If you're looking for something typically Scottish, you'll be spoiled for choice whatever your budget. Woollens, tartans, tweeds and cashmeres are everywhere, and smaller stores sell designer knitted goods in rainbow hues, or tartan with a twist, bringing Scottish style right into the 21st century. Tartan can be found in

*From traditional to whacky, designer to vintage— Edinburgh has it all*

---

**MARKETS**

Sunday sees thousands of locals heading out to Ingliston, which is home to a huge, cheap and vibrant outdoor market with more than 100 stands and a car boot sale thrown in. Undercover markets include the rambling New Street Sunday Market in the Old Town. For the best in Scottish produce, the bi-monthly Saturday Farmers' Market, held on Castle Terrace, is worth a trawl for superb organic meat, vegetables and other foods.

the form of everything from a blanket to a kilt. Local craftsmen are celebrated for their silver, metalwork and jewellery, and you'll find samples at the swanky city stores or among dozens of tiny studio-workshops. You can find the country's musical heritage in a huge range of CDs—everything from reels and pipe-and-drum music to Celtic rock and traditional Gaelic song. Books, posters and calendars make great souvenirs and gifts, and you'll find an excellent selection in many book and gift shops. As a capital city, Edinburgh is also well endowed with expensive antiques shops and fine art and contemporary galleries, while other shops specialize in historic maps and antiquarian books with a Scottish theme. Urban sophisticates can bypass all this to home in on furniture and *objets d'art* that combine traditional craftsmanship with cutting-edge design, not just from Scotland but also from all over the world.

## A Taste of Scotland

Food is always a popular souvenir, and shops sell the best of the country's produce, often vacuum-packed to make transportation easier. Choose from wild smoked salmon, Orkney cheese, heather honey and soft fruit jam, shortbread, oatcakes and a bottle of finest malt whisky from the huge range you'll find—some of which are 100 years old.

### SHOPPING AREAS

The city's retail heart beats in Princes Street, and if you're looking for chain stores it's the best choice; if not, with the exception of the excellent department store Jenners, it can be avoided. For souvenirs, head for the Old Town, where tartan, tat, sweaters and whisky crowd the shelves. The New Town's best shops are around Queen Street, with big-name, classy shopping at The Walk (▷ 79) off St. Andrew's Square—home to the beautiful Harvey Nicols. For good local shops, head for Stockbridge, Bruntsfield and Morningside. Up and coming is William Street, in the city's West End, with some great specialist shops.

# Shopping by Theme

Whether you're looking for a department store, a quirky boutique, or something in between, you'll find it all in Edinburgh. On this page shops are listed by theme. For a more detailed write-up, see the individual listings in Edinburgh by Area.

## ART AND ANTIQUES

Adam Antiques (▷ 78)
Amber Antiques (▷ 38)
Anthony Woodd Gallery (▷ 78)
Bow Well (▷ 38)
Byzantium (▷ 38)
Carson Clark (▷ 62)
Pine & Old Lace (▷ 39)
Randolph Gallery (▷ 80)

## BOOKS AND MUSIC

Analogue (▷ 38)
Bagpipes Galore (▷ 62)
Blackwell (▷ 38)
McNaughtan's Bookshop (▷ 79)
Old Town Bookshop (▷ 39)
Waterstone's (▷ 80)

## CASHMERE AND WOOL

Belinda Robertson (▷ 78)
The Cashmere Store (▷ 38)
Designs on Cashmere (▷ 62)
Frontiers (▷ 62)
Hawick Cashmere Company (▷ 39)
James Pringle Weavers (▷ 104)
Jane Davidson (▷ 79)
Linzi Crawford (▷ 79)
Ragamuffin (▷ 62)

## FOOD AND DRINK

Baxters (▷ 104)
Demijohn (▷ 38)
Ian Mellis (▷ 39)
Fudge Kitchen (▷ 62)
Peckhams (▷ 104)
Royal Mile Whiskies (▷ 39)
William Cadenhead (▷ 62)
Valvona & Crolla (▷ 80)

## GIFTS AND SOUVENIRS

Cigar Box (▷ 38)
Edinburgh Crystal Visitor Centre (▷ 104)
Halibut & Herring (▷ 39)
Fling (▷ 78)
Mr Wood's Fossils (▷ 39)
Molton Brown (▷ 79)
National Gallery of Scotland (▷ 79)
Studio One (▷ 80)
Ye Olde Christmas Shoppe (▷ 62)

## JEWELLERY

Hamilton & Inches (▷ 78)
Joseph Bonnar (▷ 79)
Palenque (▷ 62)
The Tappit Hen (▷ 62)

## LEATHER AND SHOES

Helen Bateman (▷ 79)
Mackenzie Leather Goods (▷ 39)

## SCOTTISH CLOTHING

Anta (▷ 38)
Armstrongs (▷ 38)
Geoffrey (Tailor) Kiltmakers (▷ 62)
Hector Russell (▷ 79)
Kinloch Anderson (▷ 104)
Stewart Christie & Co. (▷ 80)

## STORES AND MALLS

Frasers (▷ 78)
Harvey Nichols (▷ 78)
Jenners (▷ 79)
Gyle Shopping Centre (▷ 104)
Leith Market (▷ 104)
Ocean Terminal (▷ 104)
Princes Mall (▷ 80)
St. James Centre (▷ 80)

## OUTDOOR CLOTHING

Dickson & MacNaughton (▷ 78)
Tiso (▷ 80)

# Edinburgh by Night

In summer the city fairly buzzes with all the activities of the festivals and their fringes, catering for every taste and budget. However, there's plenty to do at any time of the year.

## Music, Theatre, Dance and Film

Outside the Festival, Edinburgh has a year-round schedule of the performing arts, with plays, music, opera, dance, ballet, comedy, folk music, rock and jazz all on offer, while cinemas show blockbusters and art-house movies. You can find listings information in *The List*, a fortnightly magazine that details every type of entertainment. Tickets for major performances can be booked through Ticketmaster (020 7344 4000; www.ticketmaster.co.uk) in the Visit Scotland office (3 Princes Street, Mon–Sat 9–5, Sun 10–5) or at venues.

## Calmer Pleasures

If you're looking for a quieter evening, the city looks fantastic after dark, with many landmark buildings illuminated. Except for the Festival weeks, restaurants in Edinburgh tend to wind down around 10pm, so don't expect to find much open later; eat around 8pm, then head for a stylish bar or traditional pub.

## Dance the Night Away

Edinburgh's club scene is far more subdued than that of Glasgow, London or Manchester, and, as in many other cities, is often in a state of flux, with venues and clubs changing from one month to the next. Friday and Saturday are the big nights, when admission prices rise and places stay open later. Check out *The List* or the free Thursday sheet *Metro*.

*Edinburgh is full of diverse opportunities for classical, traditional and trendy nights out*

### HOGMANAY

Hogmanay is Scotland's New Year, and Edinburgh celebrates it in style with a four-day spectacle that includes concerts, street parties, live music, marching bands, processions and spectacular fireworks. Some 100,000 tickets are issued by ballot in October.

# Eating Out

The culinary explorer can be spoiled for choice in cosmopolitan Edinburgh. You don't have to look hard for traditional Scottish cuisine, but there are a host of alternatives to be found from Thai and Indian to Turkish and Moroccan.

## Where and When to Eat

Restaurants reflect the diversity of British culture and there are options to suit most tastes and pockets. The one thing many have had in common until recently is their opening hours—between 12 and 2, and from 6 until 9—but this is changing, with more restaurants opening for longer hours. Many top restaurants are based in hotels but you need not be staying at the hotel to enjoy the cuisine, although it is best to book in advance. Traditional teashops are excellent for snacks and are usually open from mid-morning until 4 or 5pm. There are some good options in the larger department stores for light lunches and tea- and coffee breaks.

## International Dining

Although well-cooked, fresh, traditional food is having something of a renaissance in Scotland, the British public are always eager to sample ethnic menus. In Edinburgh you can find a good range of international restaurants, among which are many long-standing Italian treasures. With the influx of Italian immigrants to Scotland in the early 20th century, you will find good pasta and, of course, the quintessential Italian-made ice cream.

### SCOTTISH SELECTION

**Arbroath smokies**—small hot-smoked haddock.
**clootie dumpling**—steamed sweet and spicy pudding, traditionally cooked in a cloth.
**cranachan**—raspberries, cream and toasted oatmeal
**crowdie**—light curd cheese.
**Cullen skink**—creamy fish broth based on 'Finnan haddie' or smoked haddock.
**Forfar bridie**—pasty made with beef, onion and potato.

*Eating alfresco is catching on in Britain, even in this northern city*

# Restaurants by Cuisine

There are restaurants to suit all tastes and budgets in Edinburgh. On this page they are listed by cuisine. For a more detailed description of each restaurant, see Edinburgh by Area.

### BISTROS/BRASSERIES

All Bar One (▷ 84)
Blue Bar Café (▷ 42)
Circus Wine Bar & Grill (▷ 84)
Dome (▷ 84)
Doric Tavern (▷ 84)
Hadrian's Brasserie (▷ 85)
Le Sept (▷ 43)
Rogue (▷ 43)
Shaws Bistro & International Tapas Bar (▷ 44)

### FINE DINING

Number One (▷ 86)
Off the Wall (▷ 64)
Restaurant at the Bonham (▷ 106)
Rhubarb (▷ 106)
Vermilion (▷ 44)

### FISH/SEAFOOD

Creelers (▷ 42)
Mussel Inn (▷ 86)
Ship on the Shore (▷ 106)
Shore Bar & Restaurant (▷ 106)
Waterfront (▷ 106)

### INTERNATIONAL

Bellini (▷ 84)
Beluga Bar & Canteen (▷ 42)
Le Café St. Honoré (▷ 84)
Est Est Est (▷ 84)
La Garrigue (▷ 85)
Iggs (▷ 85)
Kweilin (▷ 85)
The Living Room (▷ 86)
Oloroso (▷ 86)
Pancho Villas (▷ 64)
Petit Paris (▷ 43)
La P'tite Folie (▷ 86)
Restaurant Martin Wishart (▷ 106)
Santini (▷ 44)
VinCaffè (▷ 86)

### SCOTTISH CUISINE

Atrium (▷ 42)
Deacon Brodie's Tavern (▷ 42)
Dubh Prais Restaurant (▷ 64)
Duck's at Le Marché Noir (▷ 84)
Grain Store (▷ 43)
The Grill Room (▷ 43)

Haldanes (▷ 85)
Howie's (▷ 85)
Jacksons (▷ 43)
Melrose Restaurant (▷ 86)
Stac Polly (▷ 44)
Tower Restaurant (▷ 44)
Wee Windaes (▷ 44)
Witchery by the Castle (▷ 44)

### SNACKS/LIGHT BITES

Bennets Bar (▷ 42)
Elephant House (▷ 42)
Monster Mash (▷ 43)
Olive Branch (▷ 86)
Starbank Inn (▷ 106)

### VEGETARIAN

David Bann's Vegetarian Restaurant (▷ 64, panel)
Henderson's Salad Table (▷ 85)

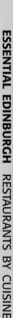

# If You Like...

However you'd like to spend your time in Edinburgh, these top suggestions should help you tailor your ideal visit. Each sight or listing has a fuller write-up in Edinburgh by Area.

## SCOTTISH SOUVENIRS

**Kilts and all things tartan** at Geoffrey Kiltmakers (▷ 62) and their Tartan Weaving Mill (▷ 35).
**Scottish pipes and music** can be found at Bagpipes Galore (▷ 62).
**A wee dram**—a huge choice of Scotland's national tipple (drink) at Royal Mile Whiskies (▷ 39).
**Edinburgh Crystal** can be found in shops in the city, but to see it made and to get a bargain go out to the Visitor Centre at Penicuik (▷ 104).

## LUXURIOUS CASHMERE

*Superior malt whisky makes a great gift*

**All you could ever desire** in this sensuous material at The Cashmere Store (▷ 38).
**Belinda Robertson** (▷ 78) produces designer cashmere products to dress the stars.
**For the very best quality** you won't go wrong if you shop at the Hawick Cashmere Company (▷ 39), but you will pay a price.
**Indulge yourself** at Designs on Cashmere (▷ 62).

## SCOTTISH FOOD

**A modern approach to Scottish cuisine** is taken at Stac Polly (▷ 44).
**Traditional dishes** are the mainstay at the intimate Wee Windaes (▷ 44).
**Enjoy top dining** and Scottish classics with a contemporary twist at the Witchery (▷ 44).
**Top Scottish cuisine** at Dubh Prais Restaurant (▷ 64) with everything from haggis to salmon.

*A taste of luxury, be it supersoft cashmere (middle) or delicious local-caught salmon (bottom)*

*When the weather's good, eat outside or take to the hills*

## INTERNATIONAL COOKING

**Cool, sleek and Italian** is the dish of the day at Est Est Est (▷ 84).

**French cuisine in Grassmarket**—Try a delightful country-style bistro in the heart of the city at Petit Paris (▷ 43).

**Look east** at the Beluga Bar & Canteen (▷ 42) for tasty Asian and Pacific Rim treats.

**A taste of Mexico** can be found at Pancho Villas (▷ 64) in Canongate.

## A BREATH OF FRESH AIR

**Classical Edinburgh** can be found at the top of Calton Hill (▷ 68).

**For some salty air** head out to Leith (▷ 94–95) and go aboard the Royal Yacht *Britannia* (▷ 97).

**In the heart of the city** stroll in the delightful Princes Street Gardens (▷ 74).

**If you are feeling energetic** get down to Holyrood Park (▷ 52) and climb up to Arthur's Seat (▷ 48–49).

## BOUTIQUE HOTELS

**From Paris to Marrakesh**—stay in a global suite at the fabulous Le Monde (▷ 111).

**Enjoy spectacular views** of Calton Hill from the comfort of your bedroom at the Glasshouse (▷ 112).

**One of the coolest hotels in town** is The Bonham (▷ 112), nicely located in New Town.

**True elegance** and sophistication can be found at The Howard (▷ 112).

*Walking the dog on Calton Hill*

*Relax in one of Edinburgh's newest boutique hotels*

*Attractions in the city range from art to animals*

## TO SAVE SOME MONEY

**Stay in a hostel** like the one in Belford Road (▷ 109).
**Buy the Edinburgh Pass** (▷ 119) if you want to see the attractions.
**Picnic in the park** at Holyrood (▷ 52) and save your lunch money.
**Visit the National Gallery** (▷ 70–71)—it's free and packed with great art.

## A KID'S DAY OUT

**See the animals** at the world-renowned zoo (▷ 92–93).
**Give yourself a scare** in the Edinburgh Dungeon (▷ 75).
**It's free** at the Museum of Childhood (▷ 54–55).
**Be hands-on** and scientific at the terrific Our Dynamic Earth (▷ 56).

## SOME ACTION

**Take a round of golf** just outside the city (▷ 105, panel).
**Enjoy a swim** at the city pool (▷ 105) or Leith Waterworld (▷ 100).
**See Scottish football** at Hearts or Hibs (▷ 105).
**Spend a day at the races**—check out the horses at Musselburgh Racecourse (▷ 105).

## GOING OUT ON THE TOWN

*The game of golf began in Scotland*

**Traditional music** can be found most nights at the Tass pub (▷ 64).
**Go clubbing** at Lulu (▷ 83), in the Tigerlily hotel.
**Boogie all night** down at club Espionage (▷ 40).
**Jamie's Scottish evening** (▷ 82) will get your feet tapping at the Thistle hotel.

*Take to the dance floor*

# Edinburgh by Area

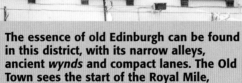

The essence of old Edinburgh can be found in this district, with its narrow alleys, ancient *wynds* and compact lanes. The Old Town sees the start of the Royal Mile, dominated by the impressive castle.

**4**

**5**

**6**

Camera Obscura
& World of Illusions

National
War Museum
of Scotland

Edinburgh
Castle

Scotch Whisky
Heritage Centre

Esplanade

Grassmarket

Canning Lane

Canning Street Lane

Canning Street Lane

Atholl Crescent Lane

LOTHIAN

West Approach Road

King's Stable Road

Castle Terrace

Cambridge Street

Royal
Lyceum
Theatre

Cornwall Street

Castle Terrace

Johnston Terrace

King's Stables Road

King's Stable Lane

West Port

Lady Lawson Street

King's Wynd

Heriot Bridge

Grassmarket

**TORPHICHEN**

St Street

Dewar Place Lane

A700

ROAD

Grindlay Street

Grindlay Street Court

Spittal Street

Cornwall Street

Bread Street

Lady Lawson Street

West Port

**7**

**MORRISON**

**STREET**

Bread Street

East Fountainbridge

Fountainbridge

High Riggs

Lauriston Street

Lauriston Place

Edinburgh
College
of Art

Chalmers Street

Archibald Place

Gardner's Street

Semple Street

Port Hamilton

**EARL GREY**

Gilmore Street

Lauriston Gardens

Lauriston Street

Glen Street

Lauriston Park

**8**

**PONTON**

**STREET**

Fire
Station

Gilmore Place

Dunbar St.

**THORNYBAUK**

**BROUGHAM**

**STREET**

Panmure Place

**BROUGHAM**

**PLACE**

West Tollcross

Lochrin Place

**HOME STREET**

Drumdryan Street

Tarvit Street

Lonsdale Terrace

P

Gilmore Place

**LEVEN**

**STREET**

Kings
Theatre

Valleyfield Street

Leven Terrace

**MELVILLE**

**DRIVE**

**9**

Hailes Street

A702

**BRUNTSFIELD PLACE**

Barony Terrace

Glengyle Terrace

*Bruntsfield Links*

0 ——— 200 m

0 ——— 200 yds

Warrender Park Terrace

**A**     **B**     **C**     **D**

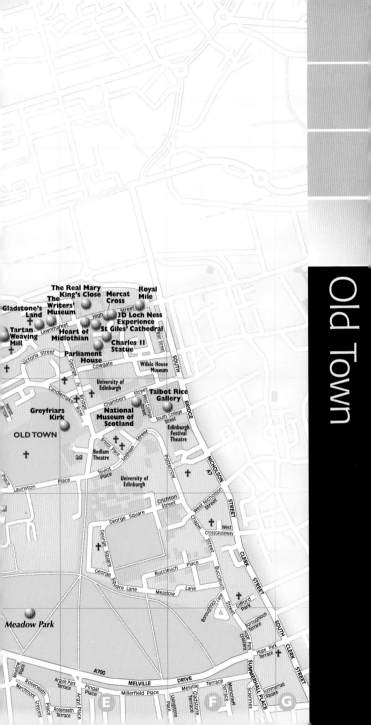

Gladstone's
Land

The Real Mary
King's Close

The
Writers'
Museum

Mercat
Cross

Royal
Mile

High Street

Tartan
Weaving
Mill

Lawnmarket

3D Loch Ness
Experience

St Giles' Cathedral

Heart of
Midlothian

Charles II
Statue

Parliament
House

Victoria Street

Cowgate

Wilkie House
Museum

George IV Bridge

Candlemaker Row

University of
Edinburgh

Chambers Street

West College Street

Talbot Rice
Gallery

BRIDGE

SOUTH

Bell Street

Greyfriars
Kirk

National
Museum of
Scotland

South College
Street

Edinburgh
Festival
Theatre

NICHOLSON ST

OLD TOWN

Bristol Place

Lothian Street

Bedlam
Theatre

Teviot
Place

University of
Edinburgh

Potterrow

Lauriston Place

Heriot Bridge

Place

Crichton
Street

West Nicholson Street

STREET

Chapel Street

West
Crosscauseway

George Square

George Square

Buccleuch
Place

CLERK

STREET

George Square Lane

Buccleuch Street

Meadow Lane

Boroughloch Lane

Gifford
Park

Meadow Park

Boroughloch
Terrace

Hope Park
Terrace

Park Road
Crescent

SOUTH

SUMMERHALL PLACE

CLERK STREET

Meadow
Place

Roseneath
Terrace

Marchmont
Crescent

Argyle Park
Terrace

Fingal
Place

A700

MELVILLE DRIVE

Millerfield Place

Melville Terrace

Livingstone
Place

Gladstone
Terrace

Moncrieff
Terrace

Summerhall
Square

Sciennes

Argyle Place

Roseneath
Place

E    F    G

# Edinburgh Castle

## HIGHLIGHTS

- Great views from the Castle Rock
- St. Margaret's Chapel
- Mons Meg
- Vaults
- Scottish Crown Jewels
- Stone of Destiny
- Scottish War Memorial
- One o' Clock Gun

## TIP

- The Esplanade in front of the castle doubles as a pay-and-display car park Nov–end May.

**Perched high on a wedge of volcanic rock, the castle is a symbol of the Scottish nation, reflecting 1,000 years of history. With its rich mix of architectural styles, it should not be missed.**

**Might and majesty** As you wind your way up the Castle Rock you can enjoy the spectacular view north over the city. The cannons along the battery were a picturesque improvement suggested by Queen Victoria. The One o' Clock Gun, a 25-pounder field gun from World War II, fires from Mills Mount Battery at precisely 1pm in a tradition dating from 1861. To enter the castle you first cross the Esplanade, the setting for the annual Military Tattoo.

**Once inside** The oldest structure in the castle is the 12th-century chapel, dedicated to St. Margaret

*Full military pageant at the annual Edinburgh Tattoo, staged at the castle (far left); stained-glass window depicting Queen Margaret inside St. Margaret's Chapel (left); the proud fortress overlooks the city (right); Megs Mon gun on the ramparts (below left); massed bands at the Tattoo (below middle); St. Margaret's Chapel (below right)*

by her son, King David I. The chapel is almost overshadowed by the huge cannon on the rampart outside—Mons Meg, a gift in 1457 to James II from the Duke of Burgundy.

**Castle of contrasts** One of the newest buildings on Castle Rock is the strikingly austere National War Memorial. Be prepared for crowds in the Crown Room, where both the Scottish Crown Jewels and The Stone of Destiny are displayed. The crown dates from 1540 and is made of Scottish gold, studded with semi-precious stones from the Cairngorms. The sword and sceptre were both papal gifts. The Stone of Destiny was the stone on which Scottish kings were crowned—pinched by Edward I, it was recovered from London's Westminster Abbey in 1996. The castle also contains the National War Museum of Scotland (▷ 33).

**THE BASICS**

www.historic-scotland.gov.uk

✚ C6

✉ Castlehill EH1 2NG

☎ 0131 225 9846

🕐 Apr–end Oct daily 9.30–6; Nov–end Mar daily 9.30–5

🍴 Cafés

🚌 23, 27, 35, 41, 42

🚉 Edinburgh Waverley

♿ Some areas are restricted, call first. A courtesy minibus is available to take less mobile people to top of castle site—check when you buy your ticket

💷 Expensive

# Greyfriars Kirk

TOP 25

*The loyal Greyfriars Bobby sits patiently outside the church and graveyard*

## THE BASICS

www.greyfriarskirk.com

**⊞** E7

**✉** Greyfriars Tolbooth and Highland Kirk, Greyfriars Place EH1 2QQ

**☎** 0131 226 5429

**🕑** Apr–end Oct Mon–Fri 10.30–4.30, Sat 10.30–2.30; Nov–end Mar Thu 1.30–3.30

**🚌** 2, 23, 27, 35, 41, 42

**🚉** Edinburgh Waverley

**♿** Very good

**💷** Free

## HIGHLIGHTS

● Greyfriars Bobby
● Elaborate 17th-century memorials
● Peaceful surroundings
● Gaelic service held at 12.30 on Sunday, when all are welcome

**Built in 1620 on the site of the garden of a former Franciscan monastery, the Kirk of the Grey Friars has had a turbulent history. Today it is a peaceful haven for quiet contemplation.**

**Battleground** Just 18 years after the church was built, it was the scene of a pivotal event in Scottish history, when Calvinist petitioners gathered to sign the National Covenant, an act of defiance against the king, Charles I. The church itself was trashed by Cromwell's troops in 1650, and later accidentally blown up. In the kirkyard a makeshift prison was erected to house hundreds of Covenanters captured after the battle of Bothwell Bridge in 1679; they were kept here for five dreadful months. Today it is full of elaborate memorials, including the grave of architect William Adam (1689–1748).

**Undying loyalty** Opposite the churchyard gate stands a popular Edinburgh landmark: a fountain with a bronze statue of a little Skye terrier, which has stood here since 1873. The dog's story was told by American Eleanor Atkinson in her 1912 novel *Greyfriars Bobby*. He was the devoted companion of a local farmer who dined regularly in Greyfriars Place. After his master died, faithful Bobby slept on his grave in the nearby churchyard for 14 years. A later version suggests he was owned by a local policeman, and taken in by local residents when his owner died. There is a portrait of Bobby, painted by John MacLeod in 1867, inside the church.

# National Museum of Scotland

*The striking Museum of Scotland incorporates the former Royal Museum*

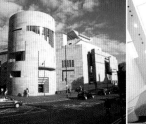

**An unashamedly modern castle protecting Scotland's national treasures. Designed by Benson & Forsyth, it incorporates the original 18th-century Royal Museum and was opened in 1998.**

**So much to see** Treasures abound in this superb collection, but it can be confusing to find your way around and you won't see it all in one visit. Work your way up chronologically from the basement through history from the earliest beginnings. Check out the section on early people, with its fascinating sculptures by Eduardo Paolozzi decked out in ancient jewels. The museum's floors follow the history of Scotland, through its Gaelic heritage, the impact of Christianity and the Union with England in 1707. Subsequent galleries display associations with culture, industry and emigration, and the impact of the Scottish nation on the world.

**Pick of the highlights** Well worth a look are the displays of the Pictish period: vivid relief carvings in stone. Don't miss the Hunterston brooch dating from around AD700, a potent symbol of wealth and power. Another highlight is the collection of 82 carved chess pieces discovered in the sands of Uig, on Lewis, in 1831; these small 12th-century greyish figures are carved from walrus ivory. Also on show are Robbie Burns' pistols.

**The future** The Royal Museum Project is an ambitious lottery-funded development to gradually reinvent the wonderful original 18th-century building for the 21st century.

## THE BASICS

www.nms.ac.uk

E7

Chambers Street EH1 1JF

0131 247 4422

Daily 10–5

Tower Restaurant (▷ 44); reservations essential at weekends. Cafés in Royal Museum building

2, 23, 27, 35, 41, 42

Very good

Free; charge for some temporary exhibitions

Check on arrival for times of free daily tours. Free audio guides available in English, Gaelic, French and German

## HIGHLIGHTS

- Pictish carvings
- Hunterston brooch
- Lewis chess pieces
- Burns' pistols
- Eduardo Paolozzi sculptures
- Great views from roof

# Royal Mile

## HIGHLIGHTS

- Narrow closes, *wynds* and *vennels* (alleys)
- Tenement houses
- Edinburgh Castle (▷ 24–25)
- Scotch Whisky Heritage Centre (▷ 31)
- St. Giles' Cathedral (▷ 30)
- Canongate Kirk (▷ 60)
- Palace of Holyroodhouse (▷ 58–59)

**Stretching downhill from Edinburgh Castle to Holyrood Palace, the Royal Mile is a focal point for visitors, who like to explore the narrow *wynds* leading off the main thoroughfare.**

**Origins of the Mile** The Royal Mile is the long, almost straight street leading up the spine of rock on which the Old Town was built. Lined with medieval tenement houses, this part of the city became so overcrowded that a New Town (▷ 72–73) had to be built in the 18th century. About 60 narrow closes, or *wynds*, lead off between the buildings on either side, with names, such as Fleshmarket, indicating the trades once carried out there.

**Down to earth** The new Scottish Parliament Building (▷ 57) dominates the Holyrood end of

*Clockwise from top left: Deacon Brodies—a traditional pub on the Royal Mile; tartan for sale at shops along the Mile; striking Old Town houses at the back of the Royal Mile; the official Royal Mile sign; on the Lawnmarket; attractive pub sign for Deacon Brodies; buildings on Cockburn Street*

THE ROYAL MILE

ABBEY STRAND

the Royal Mile. From here, the area around Canongate developed into a more practical, working district. You can see a view of the interiors of these old houses at the Museum of Edinburgh (▷ 53). Look for a board outside the Canongate Kirk (church) indicating the famous buried there.

**Onward and upward** At the crossing of St. Mary's Street and Jeffrey Street you enter High Street. Above the Tron Kirk (▷ 60) the road retains its *setts* (cobbles) and broadens out. After St. Giles' Cathedral (▷ 30), with the Heart of Midlothian (▷ 33) in the cobbles, the street becomes the Lawnmarket, with its fine 16th- and 17th-century tenements, where linen (lawn) was manufactured. The final stretch lies above the Hub (a converted church), as the road narrows on the steep approach to the castle (▷ 24–25).

**THE BASICS**

⊞ C6–H5
✉ The Royal Mile
🚌 23, 27, 35, 41, 42

**TIP**

● The route has four sections, each with its own identity. You may wish to walk it all in one go or choose to concentrate on one part.

29

# St. Giles' Cathedral

*Striking stained glass depicting biblical scenes in St. Giles' Cathedral*

## HIGHLIGHTS

● Robert Louis Stevenson memorial

● Window designed by Edward Burne-Jones

● Robert Burns window

● Stained glass

● John Knox statue

● Medieval stonework

**Imposing, and its dark stonework somewhat forbidding, the High Kirk of Edinburgh stands near the top of the Royal Mile. It is dedicated to St. Giles, the patron saint of the city.**

**Origins of the building** The columns inside the cathedral that support the 49m (160ft) tower, with its distinctive crown top, are a relic of the 12th-century church that once occupied this site. The tower itself dates from 1495, and the rest of the church from the 15th and 16th centuries. This tower is one of the few remaining examples of 15th-century work to be seen in High Street today. Much of the church has been altered and reworked over subsequent centuries. Don't miss the exquisitely carved 19th-century Thistle Chapel.

**Saintly beginnings** St. Giles' parish church—it became a cathedral in the mid-17th century—was probably founded by Benedictine followers of Giles. He was a 7th-century hermit (and later abbot and saint) who lived in France, a country with strong ties with Scotland. In 1466, the Preston Aisle of the church was completed, in memory of William Preston, who had acquired the arm bone of the saint in France. This relic disappeared in about 1577, but St. Giles' other arm bone is still in St. Giles' Church, Bruges.

**Famous sons** Presbyterian reformer John Knox (c1513–72) became minister here in 1559. You can also see a bronze memorial to writer Robert Louis Stevenson (1850–94), who died in Samoa.

# Scotch Whisky Heritage Centre

**Whisky is synonymous with Scotland and here you can learn about its 300-year history. Interactive displays let you experience related sights, sounds and smells, and you get a wee dram, too.**

**Whisky galore** This popular attraction is located at the top of the Royal Mile immediately below the castle. Learn everything there is to know about Scotland's national drink on a tour that sets off every 15 minutes and lasts around an hour. The voyage of discovery takes in a short film, a slow-moving barrel ride through history, and a talk through the manufacturing process. With models and a 'ghost'—a Master Blender from 150 years ago—it's a better all-round family fun experience than most distillery tours, which can be very technical. Adults get a free taste (juice for children), and you can then, if you are up to it, explore more than 270 whiskies and liqueurs at the Whisky Barrel Bar.

**On the whisky trail** The problem with whisky-making is that it is not a dramatic process. It takes patience and time. Fortunately the Scotch Whisky Heritage Centre injects fun into the subject with its high-tech talking tableaux and commentary, all viewed while riding along on a hollowed-out whisky barrel. En route you will come face to face with the characters who shaped the Scotch whisky industry. Delve into the intricate secrets of whisky-making, including 'nosing'—how smell can influence the way you perceive taste—and blending. The whole process is shown by the mechanical model built to represent Tormore Distillery.

## THE BASICS

www.whisky-heritage.co.uk

✚ D6

✉ 354 Castlehill, The Royal Mile EH1 2NE

☎ 0131 220 0441

🕐 May–end Sep daily 9.30–6.30; Oct–end Apr daily 10–6 (last tour 1 hour before closing)

🍽 Amber Restaurant

🚌 23, 27, 35, 41, 42

🚉 Edinburgh Waverley

♿ Very good

💷 Expensive

## HIGHLIGHTS

● Barrel ride
● Meet the whisky ghost
● Mechanical distillery model
● Tasting a dram

# More to See

### CAMERA OBSCURA AND WORLD OF ILLUSIONS

www.camera-obscura.co.uk

You'll find the Camera Obscura at the top of the Royal Mile in a castellated building known as the Outlook Tower. The camera obscura, invented in the 19th century, is like a giant pin-hole camera, with no film involved. It projects onto a viewing table a fascinating panorama of the city outside. Take a look through the Superscope, the most powerful telescope in Britain. It's best to visit on a clear day to get the ultimate view.

🔁 D6 ✉ Castlehill EH1 2ND ☎ 0131 226 3709 🕓 Jul–end Aug daily 9.30–7.30; Apr–end Jun, Sep–end Oct 9.30–6; Nov–end Mar 10–5 🚌 23, 27, 35, 41, 42 🚉 Edinburgh Waverley ♿ None 💷 Expensive

### CHARLES II STATUE

This splendid memorial to Charles II (1630–85) is the oldest statue in the city and the oldest equestrian statue in Britain. Made of lead, and erected in 1685, the sculptor is unknown.

🔁 E6 ✉ Parliament Square 🚌 23, 27, 35

### GLADSTONE'S LAND

www.nts.org.uk

This highlight in the Old Town is the re-creation of a 17th-century tenement. It emphasizes the cramped Old Town conditions—the only space for expansion was up and the building's eventual height of six floors reflects the status of its merchant owner, Thomas Gledstanes, who extended the existing tenement in 1617.

The National Trust for Scotland has re-created 17th-century shop-booths on the ground floor, where there are original painted ceilings.

🔁 D6 ✉ 477b Lawnmarket EH1 2NT ☎ 0131 226 5856 🕓 Apr–end Jun, Sep–end Oct daily 10–5; Jul–Aug daily 10–7 🚌 23, 27, 35, 41, 42 🚉 Edinburgh Waverley ♿ Few, call for details 💷 Moderate

### GRASSMARKET

A long open space below the castle rock, the Grassmarket was first chartered as a market in 1477, with corn and cattle sold here for nearly 300 years. It was also the site of public executions. A stone marks the location

*Guarding the entrance to Gladstone's Land*

*Interesting shops can be found in Victoria Street, off Grassmarket*

of the old gibbet and commemorates the Covenanting martyrs who died here. Smartened up in recent years, it now has many good shops and eating places, and the ancient White Hart Inn.

✚ D7 ✉ Grassmarket 🚌 2, 35

### HEART OF MIDLOTHIAN

With your back to the entrance of St. Giles' Cathedral, move 20 paces forward and slightly to the right, look down and you will see the outline of a heart in the cobblestones. This Heart of Midlothian marks the place of the old Tolbooth prison, where executions took place. Local custom is to spit on this spot!

✚ E6 ✉ High Street EH1 1RE 🚌 35
🚉 Edinburgh Waverley

### MEADOW PARK

Known as the Meadows, the paths and tree-planted areas make this an ideal place to wander away from the hustle of the city; although not such a good place to be at night. It's very much a locals' hangout—students from the university, doctors and nurses from

the nearby Royal Infirmary and families from the surrounding district all mingle here. It has a children's playground.

✚ D9 ✉ Meadow Park 🚌 3, 3A, 5, 7, 31
♿ Good

### MERCAT CROSS

Located outside St. Giles' Cathedral, the cross was traditionally the chosen location for public declarations, gatherings and executions. The present version, dating from the 1880s, is fashioned on the 17th-century cross. There may have been a cross here since the 12th century, when it was a focus of trade.

✚ E6 ✉ High Street 🚌 23, 27, 35, 41, 42
🚉 Edinburgh Waverley

### NATIONAL WAR MUSEUM OF SCOTLAND

www.nms.ac.uk

Exploring more than 400 years of Scottish military history in the imposing setting of Edinburgh Castle, this museum has displays ranging from major events in Scottish warfare down to the personal—diaries, private photographs and belongings of ordinary soldiers.

*The Heart of Midlothian*

*Mercat Cross*

Highlights include a pipe given by a German soldier to a sergeant in the Scots Guards on Christmas Day 1914; a vast array of weaponry; gallantry medals; and even three elephant's toes.

✚ C6 ✉ Edinburgh Castle, Castle Hill EH1 2NG ☎ 0131 247 4413 🕐 Daily 9.45–5.45 (closes 4.45 Nov–end Mar) ♿ Good 💷 Expensive (as part of ticket for castle) 🚌 23, 27, 35, 41, 42 🚉 Edinburgh Waverly

## PARLIAMENT HOUSE

The heart of the Scottish legal system, home to the law courts. Dating from the 17th century, it has a fine old hammerbeam roof and a lovely 19th-century stained-glass window. It was home to Parliament from 1639 to 1707 and again from 1999 to 2004.

✚ E6 ✉ Parliament Square EH1 1RF ☎ 0131 225 2595 🕐 Mon–Fri 9–5 🚌 23, 27, 35, 41, 42 🚉 Edinburgh Waverley ♿ Good 💷 Free

## THE REAL MARY KING'S CLOSE

www.realmarykingsclose.com

Remnants of 17th-century houses, part of the rabbit warren of the Old Town,

have been preserved beneath the City Chamber, which was built over the top in 1753. Archaeological research in 2002–3 showed evidence of the people who lived here up to the 20th century. Guided tours underground bring the close and its people to life.

✚ E6 ✉ 2 Warriston's Close, High Street EH1 1PG ☎ 0870 243 0160 🕐 Apr–end Oct daily 10–9 (Aug 9–9); Nov–end Mar Sun–Fri 10–4, Sat 10–9 🚌 23, 27, 35, 41, 42 🚉 Edinburgh Waverley ♿ Few, phone for details 💷 Expensive

## TALBOT RICE GALLERY

www.trg.ed.ac.uk

Within the University of Edinburgh, this gallery was established in 1975 and hosts changing exhibitions showcasing Scottish art and the work of international artists. There is also the fine permanent Torrie collection of Dutch and Italian Old Masters.

✚ F7 ✉ Old College, South Bridge EH8 9YL ☎ 0131 650 2210 🕐 Tue–Sat 10–5; daily during Festival 🚌 3, 7, 8, 14, 33 🚉 Edinburgh Waverley ♿ Good 💷 Free; charge for some exhibitions

*Checking out the displays in the National War Museum of Scotland*

*Back in time at the Real Mary King's Close*

## TARTAN WEAVING MILL

www.geoffreykilts.co.uk

From sheep to finished garment, learn about the process of making a kilt—and try the loom. You can buy all manner of highland dress and accessories here, too. In addition, there is information about clans and their tartans.

➕ D6 ✉ 555 Castlehill EH1 2ND 🕐 0131 226 1555 🕐 Mon–Sat 9–5.30, Sun 10–5.30 (every day until 6.30 in summer) 🚌 23, 27, 41, 42 🚆 Edinburgh Waverley ♿ Good 💷 Free exhibition; tours (Mon–Fri) moderate

## THE WRITERS' MUSEUM

www.cac.org.uk

The narrow 17th-century Lady Stair's House is home to The Writers' Museum and dedicated notably to Robert Burns (1759–96), Walter Scott (1771–1832) and Robert Louis Stevenson (1850–94). Scott and Stevenson were both born in Edinburgh, and both studied law at the university. Particularly significant is Stevenson's memorabilia, as he died abroad and there is no other museum dedicated to him. Contemporary Scottish authors are also represented.

➕ E6 ✉ Lady Stair's Close, Lawnmarket, Royal Mile EH1 2PA 🕐 0131 529 4901 🕐 Mon–Sat 10–5; also Sun 12–5 in Aug 🚌 35 🚆 Edinburgh Waverley ♿ Phone for details 💷 Free

## 3D LOCH NESS EXPERIENCE

www.3dlochness.com

Does the legend of the Loch Ness monster fascinate you? This is the place to visit before you take a trip up to the loch itself. Located next to St. Giles' Cathedral in High Street, the show is in the same premises as Highland Experience Tours (🕐 0131 226 1414), where you can book your tour to the loch itself. While you may not get Disney standard, the story and mystery surrounding the sightings of Nessie continue to absorb. Make up your own mind.

➕ E6 ✉ 1 Parliament Square, High Street EH1 1RE 🕐 0131 225 2290 🕐 Daily from 9.30–5.30 (10–5.30 in winter); performances start every 20 minutes but are subject to change 🚌 23, 27, 35, 41 🚆 Edinburgh Waverley ♿ Good 💷 Moderate

*Crossing the spectrum—tartan comes in all shades*

*Robert Burns' memorabilia on display at The Writers' Museum*

# A Wander Around the Old Town

Take in some of the highlights off the beaten track away from the main hub and get a glimpse of the buildings of the Old Town.

**DISTANCE:** 2km (1 mile)  **ALLOW:** 45 minutes' walk but more time with stops

WALK

OLD TOWN

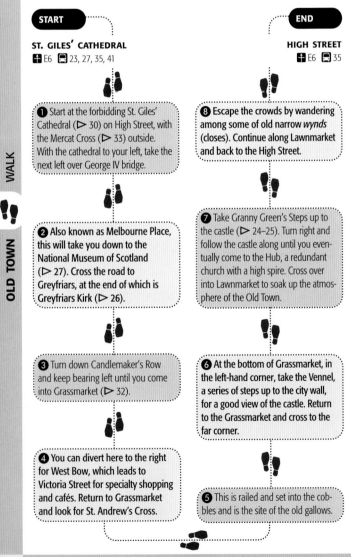

**START**

**ST. GILES' CATHEDRAL**
✚ E6  🚌 23, 27, 35, 41

**END**

**HIGH STREET**
✚ E6  🚌 35

**1** Start at the forbidding St. Giles' Cathedral (▷ 30) on High Street, with the Mercat Cross (▷ 33) outside. With the cathedral to your left, take the next left over George IV bridge.

**2** Also known as Melbourne Place, this will take you down to the National Museum of Scotland (▷ 27). Cross the road to Greyfriars, at the end of which is Greyfriars Kirk (▷ 26).

**3** Turn down Candlemaker's Row and keep bearing left until you come into Grassmarket (▷ 32).

**4** You can divert here to the right for West Bow, which leads to Victoria Street for specialty shopping and cafés. Return to Grassmarket and look for St. Andrew's Cross.

**8** Escape the crowds by wandering among some of old narrow *wynds* (closes). Continue along Lawnmarket and back to the High Street.

**7** Take Granny Green's Steps up to the castle (▷ 24–25). Turn right and follow the castle along until you eventually come to a redundant church with a high spire. Cross over into Lawnmarket to soak up the atmosphere of the Old Town.

**6** At the bottom of Grassmarket, in the left-hand corner, take the Vennel, a series of steps up to the city wall, for a good view of the castle. Return to the Grassmarket and cross to the far corner.

**5** This is railed and set into the cobbles and is the site of the old gallows.

# Shopping

## ANALOGUE
www.analoguebooks.co.uk
A bookshop with a difference that stocks design and contemporary culture books, and also a selection of magazines, music, posters and T-shirts.
➕ D6 ✉ 102 West Bow EH1 2HH ☎ 0131 220 0601 🚌 2, 23, 27,41

## AMBER ANTIQUES
Housed in a room of Gladstone's Land (▷ 32) with an original 17th-century painted ceiling. Mostly small curios of silver, porcelain and glass. Also jewellery.
➕ E6 ✉ 477 Lawnmarket EH6 4PY ☎ No phone; email: amberantiques@blueyonder.co.uk 🚌 2, 23, 27, 41, 42

## ANTA
www.anta.co.uk
Highland-made and designed fabrics, throws and cushions in wool and tweed in trendy and classic tartans. Also stoneware, tiles and luggage.
➕ D6 ✉ Crockets's Land, 91–93 West Bow EH1 2JP ☎ 0131 225 4616 🚌 2, 23, 27, 41

## ARMSTRONGS
Established in 1840, museum-like Armstrongs is well known as Scotland's largest emporium of sassy, retro and traditional Scottish clothing. There is another branch at 66 Clerk Street.
➕ D7 ✉ 83 Grassmarket EH1 2HJ ☎ 0131 220 5557 🚌 2

## BLACKWELL
www.bookshop.blackwell.co.uk
This large company, with several branches throughout Edinburgh, has been providing a comprehensive range of general and academic books and publications for more than 150 years.
➕ F7 ✉ 53–62 South Bridge Street EH1 1YS ☎ 0131 622 8222 🚌 3, 5, 7, 14, 29, 30, 31, 33, 37, 49

## BOW WELL
This small shop is crammed with all things Scottish, including the odd antler, jewellery, weapons, Highland dress, clocks, silver, paintings, ceramics and glass, plus unusual medical and scientific equipment.
➕ D6 ✉ 103–105 West Bow EH1 2JP ☎ 0131 225 3335 🚌 2, 23, 27, 41

### SCOTTISH WOOL
If you're looking for the very best in Scottish woollen items, you could spend a small fortune on designer cashmere in Edinburgh, but equally, you'll find a plethora of factory outlets with good-quality knitwear at knock-down prices, particularly cashmere. However, you are unlikely to find anything leading the way in designer fashion at the mill outlets. Serious knitters will delight in the huge range of yarns available in every conceivable shade, at a good price.

## BYZANTIUM
Go through an arched doorway to discover 15 stands, spread over two floors, bursting with antiques, books, prints and lots more, where you can unearth a treasure or just browse for the fun of it.
➕ D6 ✉ 9 Victoria Street EH1 2HE ☎ No phone 🚌 2, 23, 27, 35, 41

## THE CASHMERE STORE
www.cashmerestore.com
Come to this store, just off the Royal Mile, for a touch of luxury. Anything you could want in cashmere is here—sweaters, cardigans, scarves, dresses and skirts.
➕ E6 ✉ 2 St. Giles Street EH1 1PT ☎ 0131 225 5178 🚌 35 and all North Bridge buses

## CIGAR BOX
Every conceivable cigar can be found at this Royal Mile retailer that has achieved the Gold Standard in Habanos. From famous names like Montecristo and Romeo y Julieta to cigars from as far afield as Honduras, Nicaragua and beyond.
➕ E6 ✉ 361 High Street EH1 1PW ☎ 0131 225 3534 🚌 35 and all North Bridge buses

## DEMIJOHN
www.demijohn.co.uk
A liquid deli where you are encouraged to taste the products and personalize them with your

choice of bottle; liqueurs, spirits, whisky, oils, vinegars and spices from around the world.

🏠 D6 ✉ 32 Victoria Street EH1 2JW ☎ 0131 225 3265 🚌 2, 23, 27, 41

### HALIBUT & HERRING

For a gift with a difference head to this small shop. Heavenly smells tempt you to browse the huge selection of bathtime products, such as handmade soaps, bath bombs and toilet bags.

🏠 D6 ✉ 89 West Bow EH1 2JP ☎ 0131 226 7472 🚌 2, 23, 27, 41

### HAWICK CASHMERE COMPANY

www.hawickcashmere.com
Cashmere doesn't come cheap and a sweater from this shop starts at £100—the 'Cashmere Made In Scotland' label attached to each garment satisfies that the clothes are of the highest quality. Also sweaters and scarves.

🏠 D7 ✉ 71–81 Grassmarket EH1 2HJ ☎ 0131 225 8634 🚌 2

### IAN MELLIS

www.ijmellischeesemonger.com
Lovers of cheese owe it to themselves to visit this cheesemonger, where taste comes first. The range of Scottish cheeses is overwhelming, but staff will help find the perfect cheese for your palate.

🏠 D6 ✉ 30a Victoria Street EH1 2JW ☎ 0131 226 6215 🚌 2, 23, 27, 41

### MACKENZIE LEATHER GOODS

www.mackenziebags.co.uk
Wonderfully crafted leather bags, suitcases and other items of a very high quality.

🏠 D6 ✉ 34 Victoria Street EH1 2JW ☎ 0131 220 0089 🚌 2, 23, 27, 41

### MR WOOD'S FOSSILS

www.mrwoodsfossils.co.uk
A unique shop selling, and still unearthing, fossils of all types, both plants and animals. Founded in 1983, it first supplied museums but now specializes in retailing fossils, crystals and

minerals from Scotland and all over the world. Knowledgeable and friendly staff will fill you in on Lizzie, the oldest reptile ever discovered.

🏠 D7 ✉ 5 Cowgatehead EH1 1JY ☎ 0131 220 1344 🚌 2, 23, 27, 41, 42

### OLD TOWN BOOKSHOP

www.oldtownbookshop.com
Secondhand books on Scotland and Scottish writers, plus poetry, music, travel, art and lots more. Also a wide selection of prints and maps.

🏠 D6 ✉ 8 Victoria Street EH1 2HG ☎ 0131 225 9237 🚌 2, 23, 27, 41

### PINE & OLD LACE

Sweet little shop dealing in antique lace and linen dating from the Victorian period; all attractively displayed on old pine furniture.

🏠 D6 ✉ 46 Victoria Street EH1 2JW ☎ 0131 225 3287 🚌 2, 23, 27, 35, 41

### ROYAL MILE WHISKIES

www.royalmilewhiskies.com
Enthusiasts are on hand to offer advice on the hundreds of single malt whiskies stocked here—some are 100 years old and some are rare. Have your items shipped home, or order by phone or online.

🏠 E6 ✉ 379 High Street EH1 1PW ☎ 0131 225 3383 🚌 23, 27, 35, 41, 42

# Entertainment and Nightlife

ENTERTAINMENT AND NIGHTLIFE

OLD TOWN

## BELUGA

Opulent and stylish restaurant (▷ 42) by day where the basement bar evolves into a heaving dance floor by night. Leather seats and metal fittings, dominated by a huge waterfall.
➕ E7 ⬚ 30a Chambers Street EH1 1HU ☎ 0131 624 4545 🕐 5.30pm–1am
🚌 23, 27, 35

## BOW BAR

www.bowbar.com
If it's a wee dram you're after, this traditional pub is the place for whisky, with over 140 malts. Wood panels, old brewery mirrors and a warm greeting create an authentic atmosphere.
➕ D6 ⬚ 80 West Bow EH1 2HH ☎ 0131 226 7667
🚌 23, 27, 41

## CABARET VOLTAIRE

www.thecabaretvoltaire.com
Housed in old subterranean vaults in the Cowgate district, this club is a twin-roomed venue hosting some great gigs. All types of music, with some 30 live acts a month.
➕ E6 ⬚ 36 Blair Street EH1 1QR ☎ 0131 220 6176
🚌 5, 7, 14, 29, 35, 37
🕐 Nightly (check for times)

## CAMEO

www.picturehouses.co.uk
Small, comfortable cinema showing low-key Hollywood, international and independent films.
➕ B8 ⬚ 38 Home Street

EH3 9LZ ☎ 0870 751 5123 (booking line); 0131 228 2800 (24-hour recorded information) 🚌 10, 11, 15, 16, 17, 23, 27, 37

## EDINBURGH FESTIVAL THEATRE

www.eft.co.uk
The distinctive glass façade conceals one of the largest stages in Europe. Full schedule of international dance, plays, variety and comedy, from contemporary ballet to performances from the Scottish Opera.
➕ F7 ⬚ 13–29 Nicolson Street EH8 9FT ☎ 0131 529 6000 🚌 2, 3, 5, 7, 8, 14, 29, 31, 33, 37, 42, 49

---

### CELTIC MUSIC

Edinburgh pubs and dinner shows are the best places to track down a genuine Celtic music session. Celtic music originates from the seven Celtic countries—Scotland, Ireland, Wales, Isle of Man, Cornwall, Brittany and Galicia. The following city pubs have fine singers and musicians performing on a regular basis: Sandy Bells Bar (⬚ Forrest Road EH1 2QH ☎ 0131 225 2751); The Tass (⬚ Corner of High Street and St. Mary's Street EH1 1SR ☎ 0131 556 6338); The Royal Oak (⬚ Infirmary Street EH1 1LT ☎ 0131 557 2976). Dates and times can be erratic—check first.

---

## ESPIONAGE

www.espionage007.co.uk
Dance the night away at this popular complex, with its four spy-themed bars and one dance floor.
➕ D6 ⬚ 9 Victoria Street EH1 1EX ☎ 0131 477 7007
🕐 Nightly 7pm–3am (to 5am during Festival) 🚌 2, 23, 27, 41

## FILMHOUSE

www.filmhousecinema.com
Opposite the Usher Hall, this art-house cinema has three screens that feature the best in art-house and foreign-language cinema from around the globe.
➕ B7 ⬚ 88 Lothian Road EH3 9BZ ☎ 0131 228 2688 (box office); 0131 228 2689 (recorded information) 🚌 10, 11, 15, 17, 16, 34

## GREYFRIARS BOBBY

In front of Greyfriars Kirk and named after the famous dog, this wooden-fronted building houses a traditional friendly pub.
➕ E7 ⬚ 34 Candlemaker Row EH1 2QE ☎ 0131 225 8328 🚌 27, 35, 41, 42

## JOLLY JUDGE

www.jollyjudge.co.uk
Delightful little pub with 17th-century character, including a low-beamed ceiling and a wide choice of malt whiskies. Difficult to find but worth the search.
➕ D6 ⬚ 7 James Court, off Lawnmarket EH1 2PB ☎ 0131 225 2669 🚌 23, 27, 35, 41, 42

40

### KING'S THEATRE
www.eft.co.uk
One of Edinburgh's oldest theatres, housed in a handsome Edwardian building. Diverse range of shows and musicals, pantomime, comedy, plays and international opera during the Festival.
🚼 C8 ✉ 2 Leven Street EH3 9LQ ☎ 0131 529 6000 🚌 11, 15, 16, 17, 23

### LIQUID ROOM
www.liquidroom.com
Subterranean basement club that pulls in the punters to its renowned club night, which features big names and also promotes the cutting edge of music.
🚼 D6 ✉ 9c Victoria Street EH1 2HE ☎ 0131 225 2564 🕐 Varies so call for times 🚌 2, 23, 27, 35, 41

### ODEON
www.odeon.co.uk
Centrally located five-screen cinema with the latest sound sytems, showing all the big mainstream movies.
🚼 B7 ✉ 118 Lothian Road EH3 8BG ☎ 0871 224 4007 🚌 10, 11, 15, 16, 17, 34, 37

### QUEEN'S HALL
www.thequeenshall.net
In a converted church, this intimate venue offers a range of events, from jazz and blues to rock and classical music, and comedy from top-class performers. Home to the Scottish Chamber Orchestra.

🚼 F9 ✉ 89 Clerk Street EH8 9JG ☎ 0131 668 2019 🚌 3, 5, 7, 8, 29, 31, 37

### ROYAL LYCEUM THEATRE
www.lyceum.org.uk
A magnificent Victorian theatre that creates all its own shows. Contemporary and classic productions feature, as well as new works.
🚼 B7 ✉ Grindlay Street EH3 9AX ☎ 0131 248 4848 (box office) 🚌 1, 10, 11, 15, 16, 17, 22, 34

### SUBWAY
www.subwaycowgate.com
One of Edinburgh's top clubs, and the busiest, playing all the best from 1960s to '90s music; also live emerging bands.
🚼 E6 ✉ 69 The Cowgate EH1 1JW ☎ 0131 225 6766 🕐 Daily, evening until 5am (opening times vary) 🚌 23, 27, 35, 41, 42

### THOMSON'S BAR
www.thomsonsbar.co.uk
Winner of several real ale and independent beer awards, this refurbished pub has a wonderful interior packed with old adverts and mirrors.
🚼 A7 ✉ 182–184 Morrison Street EH3 8EB ☎ 0131 228 5700 🕐 Daily 12–12 🚌 2

### TRAVERSE THEATRE
www.traverse.co.uk
State-of-the-art venue next to the Usher Hall, respected for its experimental plays and dance productions; you can see hot new work by Scottish playwrights.
🚼 B7 ✉ 10 Cambridge Street EH1 2ED ☎ 0131 228 1404 🚌 10, 11, 22

### USHER HALL
www.usherhall.co.uk
A prestigious venue, which attracts the very best performers, such as José Carreras, the English Chamber Orchestra and the Moscow Philharmonic.
🚼 B7 ✉ Lothian Road EH1 2EA ☎ 0131 228 1155 🚌 1, 10, 11, 15, 16, 17, 22, 34

OLD TOWN

ENTERTAINMENT AND NIGHTLIFE

# Restaurants

## PRICES

Prices are approximate, based on a 3-course meal for one person.

£££ over £25
££ £15–£25
£ under £15

## ATRIUM (£££)

www.atriumrestaurant.co.uk
A popular sophisticated eatery in the theatre district that prides itself on a distinctive range of imaginative Scottish dishes.

✚ B7 ✉ 10 Cambridge Street EH1 2ED ☎ 0131 228 8882 🕐 Lunch, dinner; closed Sun, lunch Sat (except Aug) 🚌 10, 11, 16, 22

## BELUGA BAR & CANTEEN (£££)

Stained-glass windows throw vivid light across the wooden floor and dark walls, while a waterfall trickles in the background. The food is as contemporary as the interior, with a heavy slant toward Asian and Pacific Rim ingredients.

✚ E7 ✉ 30a Chambers Street EH1 1HU ☎ 0131 624 4545 🕐 Lunch, dinner 🚌 23, 27, 35, 41

## BENNETS BAR (£)

Popular with actors from the nearby Kings Theatre, this Victorian bar prides itself on sound simple homemade food at a good price, and 100 or so malt whiskies. The elaborate interior includes stained glass, tiles, mirrors and carved wood.

✚ B9 ✉ 8 Leven Street EH3 9LG ☎ 0131 229 5143 🕐 Bar meals: Mon–Sat noon–2, 5–8.30 🚌 11, 17, 23

## BLUE BAR CAFÉ (££)

www.bluebarcafe.com
Modern brasserie with good value and imaginative choices that incorporate many influences and tastes. If you prefer something light, try a crayfish sandwich or a bowl of white bean and chorizo soup. For a more substantial meal, there's carpaccio of beef with Parmesan cheese followed by

## TIPS FOR EATING OUT

Many Edinburgh restaurants can seat customers who walk in off the street, but if you have your heart set on eating at a particular establishment reserve a table in advance. Most restaurants are happy to serve a one- or two-course meal, if that is all you want. If you pay by credit card, when you key in your PIN you may be prompted to leave a tip. It's acceptable to ignore this and leave a cash tip instead. The normal amount, assuming you are happy with the service, is about 10–15 per cent. In Edinburgh it is fairly common for a reservation to last only a couple of hours, after which time you will be expected to vacate the table for the next sitting.

corn-fed chicken with aromatic leek risotto and bacon dressing.

✚ B7 ✉ 10 Cambridge Street EH1 2ED ☎ 0131 221 1222 🕐 Lunch, dinner; closed Sun 🚌 10, 11, 16, 22

## CREELERS (££–£££)

www.creelers.co.uk
Creelers is divided into two sections: the front less formal and decked out in cool blue and green to evoke the sea; the back a more intimate space with wooden floors and changing displays of art by young Scottish artists. Excellent fish and seafood direct from the family-owned Arran Smokehouse.

✚ E6 ✉ 3 Hunter Square EH1 1QW ☎ 0131 220 4447 🕐 Lunch, dinner 🚌 23, 35, 41

## DEACON BRODIES TAVERN (£)

This pub is a popular spot for locals and visitors alike with its traditional atmosphere. Bar snacks downstairs, restaurant upstairs. Find out more about the infamous Brodie while you sip your pint.

✚ D6 ✉ 435 Lawnmarket EH1 2NT ☎ 0131 225 6531 🕐 Daily, normal pub hours 🚌 23, 27, 35, 41, 42

## ELEPHANT HOUSE (£)

www.elephant-house.co.uk
A popular café offering snacks, light meals and a mouthwatering array of cakes, accompanied by excellent coffees and teas.

E6 ⊠ 21 George 1V Bridge EH1 1EN ☎ 0131 220 5355 🕐 Coffee, lunch, dinner 🚌 23, 27, 41, 42

### GRAIN STORE (££–£££)

www.grainstore-restaurant.co.uk

This smart restaurant has a unique setting in an 18th-century stone vaulted storeroom with archways and intimate alcoves. The well balanced menu includes such delights as saddle of venison with chestnuts and rosemary, using the very best of Scottish produce. Very tempting homemade desserts. Good set-price meals, too.

D6 ⊠ 30 Victoria Street (1st floor) EH1 2JW ☎ 0131 225 7635 🕐 Lunch, dinner 🚌 2, 23, 27, 41

### THE GRILL ROOM (£££)

www.starwoodhotels.com

The formal Grill Room focuses on local Scottish produce served with an international twist. Stark white tablecloths, sparkling silver, glistening crystal, fine bone china and an intimate atmosphere set the tone for exquisite fine dining.

B7 ⊠ Sheraton Grand Hotel, 1 Festival Square EH3 9SR ☎ 0131 229 9131 🕐 Lunch Tue–Fri, dinner Tue–Sat 🚌 1, 10, 11, 16, 34

### JACKSONS (££–£££)

www.jacksons-restaurant.co.uk

Lovely ambience in this elegant tiny restaurant near St. Giles' Cathedral. The best of ingredients are used to create a blend of traditional Scottish and international fare. Tasty meats and game as well as haggis cooked as you have never tried before. Great wines and whiskies.

E6 ⊠ 209 High Street EH1 1PE ☎ 0131 225 1793 🕐 Lunch, dinner 🚌 23, 27, 35, 41, 42

### LE SEPT (££–£££)

www.eloc.demon.co.uk

Vibrant French bistro with a light and airy feel and bright Parisian posters on the wall. Crêpes with a wide range of delicious fillings are the house special, but there are many other dishes to choose from.

E6 ⊠ 5 Hunter Square EH1 1QW ☎ 0131 225 5428

---

## PUB GRUB

Central-city dining pubs traditionally serve snacks and light meals such as sandwiches, toasted sandwiches, filled potatoes and ploughmans (bread, cheese and pickles). Nowadays many have extended their menu to such dishes as curry, steak-and-ale pie, steak and chips or even haggis and neeps (a blend of swede and potato mashed with butter and milk). But, on the whole, pub food in Scotland is not overly imaginative.

---

🕐 Lunch, dinner 🚌 23, 35, 41

### MONSTER MASH (££)

www.monstermashcafe.co.uk

Sausage and mashed potato is staging a comeback here. The bangers come in many varieties, such as Auld Reekie (smoked) and Mediterranean (with basil and sun-dried tomatoes), and there is a variety of mash, too. Plastic tomato-shaped ketchup bottles add a large helping of nostalgia. Also a branch at 47 Thistle Street.

E7 ⊠ 4a Forrest Road EH1 2QN ☎ 0131 225 7069 🕐 Breakfast, lunch, dinner 🚌 35, 45

### PETIT PARIS (££)

www.petitparis-restaurant.co.uk

France meets Scotland at this country-style bistro with blue-checked tablecloths. The cooking is genuine and features regional specialities—for example from Alsace.

D7 ⊠ 38–40 Grassmarket EH1 2JU ☎ 0131 226 2442 🕐 Tue–Sun lunch, dinner 🚌 2

### ROGUE (££)

A stylish yet affordable haunt enhanced by cool black furniture and crisp white tablecloths. Dishes include such delights as fillet of beef with black truffle and foie gras butter on spinach and noodles, or breast of guinea fowl with pilaff of red rice and salsa verde.

B7 ⊠ 67 Morrison Street

EH3 8BU ☎ 0131 228 2700
🕒 Lunch, dinner; closed Sun
🚌 2, 34, 35

## SANTINI (££–£££)

This elegant venue includes Santini Bis, an informal all-day option offering pizza, pasta and lighter dishes. The main restaurant is decorated in neutral shades with lots of glass and chrome and offers Italian dishes.
➕ B7 ✉ 8 Conference Square EH3 8AN ☎ 0131 221 7788 🕒 Lunch, dinner; closed Sun, lunch Sat 🚌 10, 11, 15, 16, 17, 22, 34

## SHAWS BISTRO & INTERNATIONAL TAPAS BAR (£–£££)

www.shawsrestaurant.com
Modern, lively and intimate, Shaws hit the dining scene in late 2005. Sip cocktails lounging on leather sofas, sample tasty tapas or dine on the cuisine of all five continents.
➕ E6 ✉ 21 Old Fishmarket Close EH1 1RW ☎ 0131 226 1300 🕒 Mon–Sat lunch, dinner 🚌 23, 27, 35, 41, 42

## STAC POLLY (££)

www.stacpolly.com
Cream parchment walls, low ceilings, red carpet and tartan-clad chairs help create an intimate atmosphere. Mostly modern Scottish cuisine with such tempting delights as baked supreme of Scottish salmon served with braised leeks, bacon dumplings and a lemon

butter sauce. Don't pass on dessert.
➕ B7 ✉ 8–10 Grindlay Street EH3 9AS ☎ 0131 229 5405
🕒 Lunch Mon–Fri, dinner daily
🚌 1, 10, 11, 15, 16, 17

## TOWER RESTAURANT (£££)

www.tower-restaurant.com
On the fifth floor of the Museum of Scotland, with great views of the castle, this chic and stylish restaurant offers an interesting selection of eclectic dishes using quality Scottish ingredients.
➕ E7 ✉ National Museum of Scotland, Chambers Street EH1 1JF ☎ 0131 225 3003

### FOOD ON THE RUN

Edinburgh has lots of quick options when you don't want to stop for long. There are food courts in shopping malls, while many attractions have their own restaurants and cafés. American fast-food chains have reached most corners of Scotland, so you won't have to look far to find a pizza or hamburger. The city is liberally sprinkled with very good take-out sandwich bars. Although Edinburgh has many traditional cafés, the word 'café' is used to describe the increasing number of more stylish Continental-style establishments, which bridge the gap between pubs, restaurants and coffee bars by selling coffees, snacks, wines and meals.

🕒 Lunch, dinner 🚌 2, 23, 27, 35, 41, 42

## VERMILION (£££)

www.thescotsmanhotel.co.uk
Intimate and distinctive, Vermilion serves simple classic dishes with a contemporary twist. Handmade glasses and decanters, leather chairs and bespoke cutlery lend an air of sophistication.
➕ E6 ✉ Scotsman Hotel, 20 North Bridge EH1 1YT ☎ 0131 556 5565 🕒 Dinner Wed–Sun 🚌 3, 5, 7, 30, 31, 33, 37

## WEE WINDAES (££)

www.weewindaes.org.uk
Gaze out over the cobbled streets of Edinburgh's Royal Mile while tucking into fine Scottish fare by candlelight. Haggis, salmon, pheasant, Angus beef and other traditional dishes are all cooked to perfection.
➕ E6 ✉ 144 High Street EH1 1QS ☎ 0131 225 5144
🕒 Lunch, dinner 🚌 23, 27, 41

## WITCHERY BY THE CASTLE (£££)

www.thewitchery.com
This enchanting candle-lit restaurant is the place for a special night out. The cooking displays a contemporary spin on Scottish classics like game, fish and shellfish. Huge selection of wines.
➕ D6 ✉ Castlehill, Royal Mile EH1 2NF ☎ 0131 225 5613 🕒 Lunch, dinner
🚌 23, 27, 35, 41, 42

**At the east end of the Royal Mile is the Canongate, culminating in the modern Scottish Parliament Building, the Palace of Holyroodhouse and the open space of Holyrood Park to relax in after sightseeing.**

Canongate and Holyrood

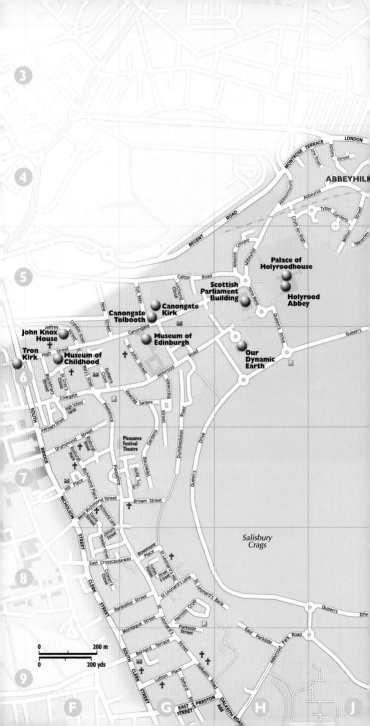

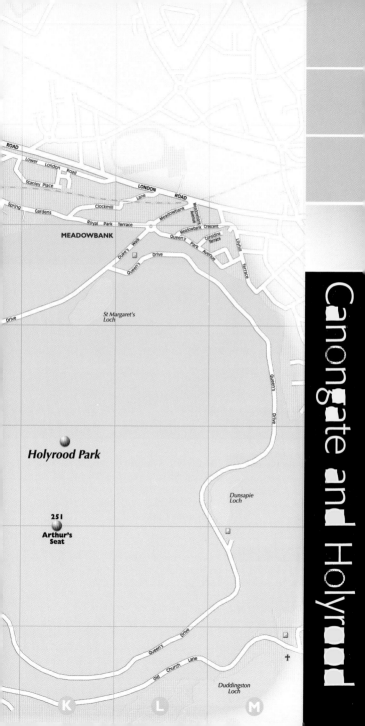

ROAD

Lower London Road

Stanley Place

LONDON ROAD

Spring Gardens

Clockmill Lane

Royal Park Terrace

Meadowbank

MEADOWBANK

Meadowbank Avenue

Duke's Walk

Queen's Park Avenue

Meadowbank Crescent

Considine Terrace

Lilyhill Terrace

Queen's Drive

St Margaret's Loch

Drive

Queen's Drive

**Holyrood Park**

**251
Arthur's
Seat**

Dunsapie
Loch

Queen's Drive

Old Church Lane

Dunsapie
Loch

Duddingston
Loch

K    L    M

Canongate and Holyrood

# Arthur's Seat

### HIGHLIGHTS

● Spectacular views
● The walk to the top
● Dunsapie Loch and bird reserve

### TIP

● Try to pick a clear day to get the best from the views. It's a waste to make the effort if it's a 'dreich' day, as the Scots call a dismal day.

**The perfect antidote to the stresses of the city, with spectacular views. Arthur's Seat is the remains of an extinct volcano 325 million years old, and it's right on Edinburgh's doorstep.**

**Geological background** The green hill of Arthur's Seat is a city landmark, 251m (823ft) high and visible for miles. Formed during the early Carboniferous era, it is surrounded by seven smaller hills. The summit marks where the cone erupted and molten rock from the volcano formed the high cliffs of Salisbury Crags. During the Ice Age, erosion exposed the twin peaks of Arthur's Seat and the Crow Hill. There are a variety of explanations for the name; some say it is a corruption of the Gaelic name for 'archers', others that the Normans associated it with King Arthur.

*Clockwise from top left: view of Salisbury Crags from the foot of Arthur's Seat; for a great view over the city it is worth the climb up to Arthur's Seat; scaling the heights; silhouette of Salisbury Crags at dusk; Arthur's Seat overlooking Edinburgh, as seen from the city's Royal Observatory on Blackford Hill*

**Get active** There is open access to Arthur's Seat, the hills and four small lochs, all of which are part of the Royal Park of Holyrood. It is worth the climb to the top for the views over the Palace of Holyroodhouse and beyond. Start your climb from a path near St. Margaret's Well, just inside the palace's entrance to the park. The path divides at the start of Hunter's Bog valley but both branches lead to the summit. The right-hand path will take you along the Radical Road that runs beneath the rock face of the Salisbury Crags. The left path goes through Piper's Walk to the top. You'll find parking at the palace, in Duddingston village and by the pools of St. Margaret's Loch and Dunsapie Loch, which has a bird reserve. From the loch it is just a short climb over some rocks to the top. From here the whole panorama of Edinburgh, plus the Firth of Forth, the Pentland hills and the coast, is below.

**THE BASICS**

✚ K7

✉ Holyrood Park

🕐 24 hours, 365 days, but no vehicular access to the park (except for Dunsapie Loch) on Sun

🚌 35 and then walk through park; or 4, 5, 44, 45 to Meadowbank and walk

🚆 Edinburgh Waverley

♿ Few

49

# Canongate Tolbooth

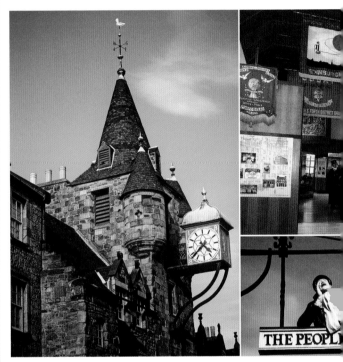

THE PEOPL

## HIGHLIGHTS

● The building
● Prison cell
● 1940s kitchen
● Cooper's workshop
● Re-created pub

## TIP

● Visit the museum early on in your trip to Edinburgh to give you an insight into the background of the people who made the city what it is today.

**Dating from 1591, this French-style Tolbooth has served as both a council chamber and a prison. It now houses the People's Story, a museum of everyday life since the 18th century.**

**From toll-house to museum** The Tolbooth is the oldest remaining building in this district and marked the boundary between Holyrood and Edinburgh proper. It served as the council chamber for the independent burgh of Canongate until its incorporation into the city in 1856. A five-floor building with a turreted steeple, it was also used as a prison for the burgh. The huge boxed clock that projects above the street was added in 1884.

**Edinburgh life** The building is now home to the People's Story, a museum dedicated to everyday

*Clockwise from top left: the turreted Canongate Tolbooth, home to the People's Story museum; trade union banners; passing the time down the pub, one of the museum's displays; the struggle for the right to vote, the people of Edinburgh on the march; all aboard—a 'clippie' model at the museum; the museum sign*

life and times in Edinburgh from the 18th century up to the present day. Using oral history, written sources and the reminiscences of local people, it creates a fascinating insight. Indulge your senses through the visual displays, sounds and smells that evoke life in a prison cell, a draper's shop and a cooper's (barrel maker's) workshop. See a servant at work and a tramcar conductor (a 'clippie', who clipped the tickets). The museum portrays the struggle for improved conditions, better health and ways to enjoy what little leisure the citizens had. The trades union movement and friendly societies played a big part in the struggle for people's rights and they feature in the museum.

**Time off** Check out the places the locals went for gossip, such as the re-created pub, the tearoom and the washhouse.

## THE BASICS

www.cac.org.uk

➕ G5

✉ 163 Canongate EH8 8BN

☎ 0131 529 4057

🕐 Mon–Sat 10–5; also Sun 12–5 in Aug

🚌 35

🚆 Edinburgh Waverley

♿ Good

🎫 Free

❓ Shop stocks a wide range of local social history books

# Holyrood Park

Arthur's Seat, at the heart of Holyrood Park (left); festival time in the park (right)

## THE BASICS

www.historic-scotland.gov.uk

🚇 K7

✉ Holyrood Park

☎ Historic Scotland Ranger Service: 0131 652 8150

🕐 24 hours, 365 days a year, but no vehicular access to the park (except for Dunsapie Loch) on Sun

🚌 35 to palace entrance; other buses to perimeter

🚆 Edinburgh Waverley

♿ Varies, phone for details

💷 Free

❓ Maps of walks available from staff in Broad Pavement car park (by Holyrood Palace and Holyrood Information Centre by the Scottish Parliament) 🕐 Daily 8.30–3.30

## HIGHLIGHTS

● Arthur's Seat (▷ 48–49)
● Dunsapie Loch
● St. Margaret's Well

**It's unusual—and a pleasant surprise—to discover a city park containing such wild countryside. You'll even find whole lochs within Edinburgh's Holyrood Park.**

**City's green treasure**  A royal park since the 12th century, Holyrood Park was enclosed by a stone boundary wall in 1541. Spreading out behind the Palace of Holyroodhouse (▷ 58–59), it extends to some 263ha (650 acres) and is dominated by the great extinct volcano, Arthur's Seat (▷ 48–49). It represents a microcosm of Scottish landscape, boasting four lochs, open moorland, marshes, glens and dramatic cliffs, the Salisbury Crags, a popular spot for rock climbers and abseilers to practise their skills.

**Get your boots on**  The park is circled by Queen's Drive, built at the instigation of Prince Albert and closed to commercial vehicles. The area around Dunsapie Loch gives a real sense of remote countryside and is a good spot to start the ascent to Arthur's Seat. It is particularly peaceful here when cars are prohibited on Sunday. Altogether Holyrood Park is an excellent place to walk, cycle or picnic.

**More to see**  Also in the park is St. Margaret's Well, a medieval Gothic structure near the palace, where a clear spring wells from beneath sculpted vaulting. Above St. Margaret's Loch, a 19th-century artificial lake, are the remains of St. Anthony's Chapel. On the edge of the park you will find Duddingston village, with one of the oldest pubs in Edinburgh, and the attractive Duddingston Loch.

*Displays at the Museum of Edinburgh, located in the Georgian Huntly House*

# Museum of Edinburgh

**The home of Edinburgh's own museum is Huntly House, a 16th-century dwelling much altered in subsequent centuries and at one time occupied by a trade guild.**

**Picturesque house** Just across the road from the Canongate Tolbooth and the People's Story (▷ 50–51), the building housing the Museum of Edinburgh is distinguished by its three pointed gables. Robert Chambers, a Victorian antiquarian, called Huntly House 'the speaking house' owing to the Latin inscriptions on the façade.

**What's on show** Inside the museum is a treasure house of local details that brings the history of the city to life. The collections include maps and prints, silver, glass and a vibrant collection of old shop signs. There is also a fine collection of Edinburgh ceramics and examples of Scottish pottery, as well as items relating to Field Marshal Earl Haig, commander of the British Expeditionary Force in World War I. Of particular interest is the collar and bowl that once belonged to Greyfriar's Bobby (▷ 26), together with the original plaster model for the bronze statue of the dog in Candlemaker Row. The museum regularly presents temporary exhibitions that further highlight aspects of local life and are drawn from the extensive local history and decorative arts collections.

**Historical Covenant** Also on show is the original National Covenant signed by Scotland's Presbyterian leadership in 1638, which is one of the city's greatest treasures.

## THE BASICS

www.cac.org.uk
+ G6
⊠ Huntly House, 142 Canongate, Royal Mile EH8 8DD
☎ 0131 529 4143
🕐 Mon–Sat 10–5; also Sun 12–5 during Aug
🚌 35
🚂 Edinburgh Waverley
♿ Poor
🎟 Free

## HIGHLIGHTS

● Huntly House building
● Greyfriar's Bobby–collar and bowl
● National Covenant
● Earl Haig memorabilia

# Museum of Childhood

## HIGHLIGHTS

● Extensive toy collection
● Re-creation of 1930s classroom
● Victorian dolls
● Dolls' houses
● Automata

## TIP

● Check in advance for the schedule of regularly changing exhibitions and varied events to get the most out of your visit.

**This has been described as 'the noisiest museum in the world' and it is popular with both children and adults. Introduce your children to the past and maybe relive it yourself.**

Nostalgic pleasure The Museum of Childhood is a delight and claims to be the first museum in the world dedicated to the history of childhood. It was the brainchild of town councillor Joseph Patrick Murray, who argued that the museum was about children rather than for them. Opened in 1955, the collection has grown to display a nostalgic treasure trove of dolls and dolls' houses, train sets and teddy bears. Every aspect of childhood is covered here, from education and medicine to clothing and food. Don't miss the re-created 1930s schoolroom—complete with the chanting

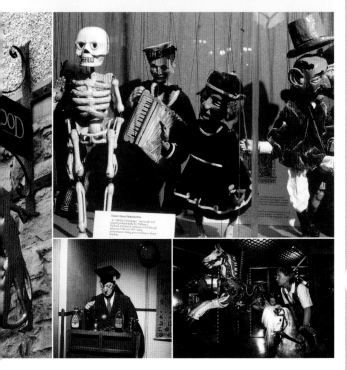

*Back to the days of rocking horses and merry-go-rounds at the delightful Museum of Childhood (left); the attractive sign beckons visitors to the museum (middle); puppet scene (right); are you paying attention? Old-fashioned schoolroom and teacher (below left); all the fun of the fair at the Museum of Childhood (below right)*

of multiplication tables, and watch the street games of Edinburgh children in the 1950s.

**Awakening memories** Adults who have never really grown up may well find nostalgic memories of the past. There is a collection of older material such as Victorian dolls and German automata, but probably the best part is recognizing the objects from your own childhood, such as Meccano. If you have children, then a visit will be enjoyable, but even without children, this museum should still be on the 'must visit' list.

**Founding father** Patrick Murray said that his museum explored a specialized field of social history. From the early days of the museum he put his own mark on the huge array of exhibits, with his slant on informative labels.

## THE BASICS

www.cac.org.uk

✚ F6

✉ 42 High Street, Royal Mile EH1 1TG

☎ 0131 529 4142

🕐 Mon–Sat 10–5, Sun 12–5

🚌 35 and all North Bridge buses

🚉 Edinburgh Waverley

♿ Very good

🎟 Free

# Our Dynamic Earth

*In the jaws of a sabre tooth tiger (left); the Restless Earth exhibition (right)*

## THE BASICS

www.dynamicearth.co.uk

🔁 H6

✉ 112 Holyrood Road
EH8 8AS

☎ 0131 550 7800

🕐 Mar–end Oct daily 10–5,
(Jul–Aug 10–6); Nov–end
Feb Wed–Sun 10–5

🍴 The Food Chain

🚌 35

🚉 Edinburgh Waverley

♿ Excellent

💷 Expensive

❓ Well-stocked gift shop–
Natural Selection

## HIGHLIGHTS

● Striking building
● Time machine
● Virtual reality helicopter
trip
● Tropical rainforest
● 'Submarine trip'
● Restless Earth experience
● FutureDome
● Earthscape Scotland

**This tented, spiky roof rising like a white armadillo on the edge of Holyrood Park is Edinburgh's Millennium project: a science park that thrills at every turn.**

**Popular science** This interactive spectacular tells the story of the Earth and its changing nature, from the so-called Big Bang (as viewed from the bridge of a space ship) to the present day (exactly who lives where in the rainforest). This is virtual reality at its slickest—great entertainment for kids, but it may prove a bit too whizzy for some.

**Stunning effects** With 12 galleries devoted to the planet, the underlying message is that the world is a fascinating and ever-changing place. Experience the effect of erupting volcanoes, the icy chill of the polar regions and even a simulated earthquake while lava apparently boils below. You may get caught in a humid rainstorm in the Tropical Rainforest. Every 15 minutes the sky darkens, lightning flashes, thunder roars and torrential rain descends. You can travel in the Time Machine, where numerous stars are created using lights and mirrors. A multiscreen flight over mountains and glaciers is a dizzying highlight. New in 2006 were Earthscape Scotland, a trip through geological time and FutureDome, an exciting interactive journey into the future.

**Plenty of stamina** Our Dynamic Earth is proving a popular, impressive feat of high-tech ingenuity. Hardly a relaxing experience, it's well worth a visit, although peak times are likely to be crowded.

*Controversial, expensive but never boring, the extraordinary Scottish Parliament Building*

# Scottish Parliament Building

**TOP 25**

**With the passing of the Scotland Act in 1998, the first Scottish Parliament since 1707 was established. It has been at this controversial building since 2004.**

**Setting the scene** From 1999, the Scottish Parliament was housed in buildings around the Royal Mile. Debating took place in the Church of Scotland Assembly at the top of the Mound. The then First Minister Donald Dewar commissioned a new parliament building to be constructed opposite Holyrood Palace. At an original estimated cost of around £40 million, the building was finally opened by the Queen in October 2004, by which time the cost had soared to over £400 million. This expense caused a good deal of controversy, but the resulting building has also attracted much praise.

**No expense spared** Hailed by architects and critics as one of the most significant new buildings in Britain, the complex was the work of Barcelona-based architect Enric Miralles. It is a unique Catalan-Scottish blend. The building is set within newly landscaped public gardens near the Palace of Holyroodhouse, against a backdrop of the Salisbury Crags. Natural materials have been carefully crafted to produce a fine level of excellence, with expert use of wood, stone and glass. Intricate details in oak and sycamore have been used throughout to offset the granite and smooth concrete finishes. The Debating Chamber, where the 129 members meet, has a striking oak-beamed ceiling. Miralles' expertise combined design with practicality through acute attention to detail.

## THE BASICS

www.scottish.parliament.uk
➕ H5
✉ The Scottish Parliament, Holyrood Road, EH99 1SP
☎ 0131 348 5200
🕐 Business days Tue–Thu 9–7. Non-business days (Mon, Fri and weekends) and when Parliament is in recess Apr–end Oct 10–6; Nov–end Mar 10–4
🍴 Café ☕ 35
🚇 Edinburgh Waverley
♿ Excellent
🎟 Free; tours moderate
❓ Guided tours lasting 1 hour are available on most non-business days. Reserve tickets for Public Gallery in advance. Shop sells exclusive items branded to the Scottish Parliament

## HIGHLIGHTS

● Architecture
● Exhibition on Scottish Parliament
● Public Gallery

# Palace of Holyroodhouse

**Founded as a monastery in 1128, today the palace is the Queen's official residence in Scotland. The pepperpot-towered castle is set against the back-drop of majestic Arthur's Seat, at the foot of the Royal Mile.**

**Steeped in royal history** In the 15th century the palace became a guesthouse for the nearby Holyrood Abbey (now a scenic ruin), and its name is said to derive from the Holy Rood, a fragment of Christ's Cross belonging to David I (c1080–1153). Mary, Queen of Scots, stayed here, and a brass plate marks where her Italian favourite, David Rizzio, was murdered in her private apartments in the west tower in 1566. During the Civil War in 1650 the palace was seriously damaged by fire and major rebuilding

Clockwise from far left: crowning glory—a royal lantern outside the Palace of Holyroodhouse; a stone unicorn guarding the palace; the mellow evening light enhances the fairytale palace; lion detail on the palace gates; a view of the palace and Arthur's Seat from Calton Hill

was necessary. Bonnie Prince Charlie held court here in 1745, followed by George IV on his triumphant visit to the city in 1822, and later by Queen Victoria en route to Balmoral.

**Home and art gallery** The palace offers all the advantages of exploring a living space steeped in history and filled with works of art from the Royal Collection. More precious artworks are on view in the stunning Queen's Gallery, by the entrance and opposite the new Scottish Parliament. The state rooms, designed by architect William Bruce (1630–1710) for Charles II and hung with Brussels tapestries, are particularly elaborate and ornately splendid. Don't miss the 110 preposterous royal portraits painted in a hurry by Jacob de Wet in 1684–86, which are hung in the Great Gallery.

**THE BASICS**

www.royal.gov.uk

✚ H5

✉ Canongate, Royal Mile EH8 8DX

☎ 0131 556 5100

🕐 Apr–end Oct daily 9.30–6; Nov–end Mar 9.30–4.30. May close at short notice

🍴 Café in old coach house

🚌 35, 36

🚉 Edinburgh Waverley

♿ Good 💷 Expensive

❓ Free audio tour available. Gift shop stocks cards, books and china

## More to See

### CANONGATE KIRK

Built in 1688, this church's distinctive Dutch gable and plain interior reflect the Canongate's trading links with the Low Countries. Note the gilded stag's head at the gable top, traditionally a gift of the monarch. Buried in the graveyard are the economist and philosopher Adam Smith (1723–90) and David Rizzio, darling of Mary, Queen of Scots, murdered in 1566. ✚ G5 ✉ Canongate EH8 8BR ☎ 0131 556 3515 🕐 Jun–end Sep Mon–Sat 10.30–4, Sun service at 11.15; burial ground open all year 🚌 35 🚉 Edinburgh Waverley ♿ Good ✋ Free (donations welcomed)

### HOLYROOD ABBEY

You can see the ruins of the abbey only on a visit to the Palace of Holyroodhouse (▷ 58–59). The present structure was built in the early 13th century. ✚ H5 ✉ The Palace of Holyroodhouse EH8 8DX ☎ 0131 556 5100 🕐 Apr–end Oct daily 9.30–6; Nov–end Mar 9.30–4.30. May close at short notice 🚌 35 🚉 Edinburgh Waverley ♿ Good ✋ Expensive

### JOHN KNOX HOUSE

Dating to the 15th century, the house is typical of the period, with overhanging gables and picturesque windows. Housed within is a museum with displays relating to Knox and to James Mosman, jeweller to Mary, Queen of Scots. The house is also home to the Scottish Storytelling Centre (▷ 64). ✚ F6 ✉ 43–45 High Street EH1 1SR ☎ 0131 556 9579 🕐 Mon–Sat 10–6, Sun (Jul–Sep only) 12–6 🚌 35 and all North Bridge buses 🚉 Edinburgh Waverley ♿ Ground floor only ✋ Moderate

### TRON KIRK

This fine early Scottish Renaissance church was built between 1637 and 1663 and stands on the Royal Mile. Its name derives from the salt-tron, a public weighbeam that once stood outside. Not used for public worship since 1952, it housed the Old Town Information Centre until 2006 and at the time of writing was closed awaiting its future use, possibly as a restaurant. ✚ E6 ✉ High Street EH1 2NG 🚌 35 and all North Bridge buses 🚉 Edinburgh Waverley

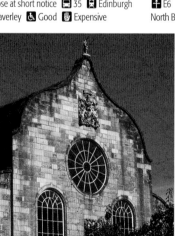

*The façade of Canongate Kirk*

*Carved sign on John Knox House*

# Through Canongate to Holyrood Park

Walk along to Canongate, with its interesting historic buildings and museums, and then take a break in the glorious Holyrood Park.

**DISTANCE:** 1.5km (1 mile) **ALLOW:** 1 hour (plus time in the park)

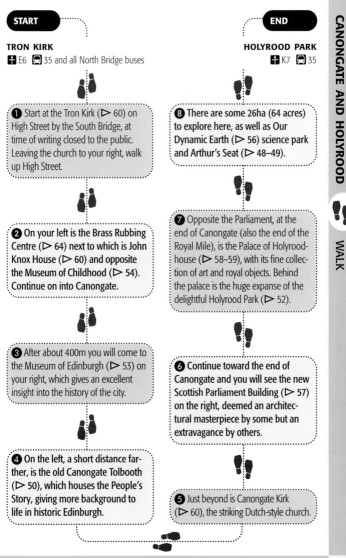

**START**

**TRON KIRK**
✚ E6 🚌 35 and all North Bridge buses

**1** Start at the Tron Kirk (▷ 60) on High Street by the South Bridge, at time of writing closed to the public. Leaving the church to your right, walk up High Street.

**2** On your left is the Brass Rubbing Centre (▷ 64) next to which is John Knox House (▷ 60) and opposite the Museum of Childhood (▷ 54). Continue on into Canongate.

**3** After about 400m you will come to the Museum of Edinburgh (▷ 53) on your right, which gives an excellent insight into the history of the city.

**4** On the left, a short distance farther, is the old Canongate Tolbooth (▷ 50), which houses the People's Story, giving more background to life in historic Edinburgh.

**END**

**HOLYROOD PARK**
✚ K7 🚌 35

**8** There are some 26ha (64 acres) to explore here, as well as Our Dynamic Earth (▷ 56) science park and Arthur's Seat (▷ 48–49).

**7** Opposite the Parliament, at the end of Canongate (also the end of the Royal Mile), is the Palace of Holyroodhouse (▷ 58–59), with its fine collection of art and royal objects. Behind the palace is the huge expanse of the delightful Holyrood Park (▷ 52).

**6** Continue toward the end of Canongate and you will see the new Scottish Parliament Building (▷ 57) on the right, deemed an architectural masterpiece by some but an extravagance by others.

**5** Just beyond is Canongate Kirk (▷ 60), the striking Dutch-style church.

61

# Shopping

### BAGPIPES GALORE
www.bagpipe.co.uk
Listen before you buy at this atmospheric shop selling Scottish-made bagpipes (▷ panel) for beginners or the more proficient. Pipe books, CDs and accessories, too.
🖽 G6 ✉ 82 Canongate EH8 8BZ ☎ 031 556 4073 🚍 35

### CARSON CLARK
This wonderful gallery specializes in antique maps and sea charts from all over the globe, dating from the 16th to 19th centuries.
🖽 G6 ✉ 181–183 Canongate EH8 8BN ☎ 0131 556 4710 🚍 35

### DESIGNS ON CASHMERE
www.designsoncashmere.com
Pamper yourself with one of these exquisite Scottish cashmere garments, for men and women. Quality comes at a price.
🖽 G6 ✉ 28 High Street EH1 1TB ☎ 0131 556 6394 🚍 35 and all North Bridge buses

### FRONTIERS
One of many woollen shops on the Royal Mile and set just below the junction with Jeffrey Street. The high quality is reflected in the prices. Handmade knitwear, including cashmere and woollen accessories, sweaters, bags and scarves.
🖽 G6 ✉ 254 Canongate EH8 8AA ☎ 0131 556 2791 🚍 35

### FUDGE KITCHEN
www.fudgekitchen.co.uk
This shop positively oozes with 20 different varieties of delectable fudge. All handmade using the finest ingredients from a recipe dating from 1830.
🖽 F6 ✉ 32 High Street EH1 1TB ☎ 0131 558 1517 🚍 35 and all North Bridge buses

### GEOFFREY (TAILOR) KILTMAKERS
www.geoffreykilts.co.uk
Specialists in traditional, casual and modern kilt-making, and outfitters for men, women and children.
🖽 F6 ✉ 57–61 High Street EH1 1SR ☎ 0131 557 0256 🚍 35 and all North Bridge buses

### PALENQUE
www.palenquejewellery.co.uk
Palenque specializes in competitively priced contemporary and silver rings, necklaces and bracelets and hand-crafted accessories.
🖽 F6 ✉ 56 High Street EH1

---

**BAGPIPES**

The bagpipes are synonymous with Scotland. You see them everywhere, from the Military Tattoo in Edinburgh to school sports days and agricultural shows. There are many types played in a variety of countries throughout the world, and, surprisingly, the bagpipes' origins are not Scottish but possibly from ancient Egypt or Greece.

---

1TB ☎ 0131 557 9553 🚍 35 and all North Bridge buses

### RAGAMUFFIN
www.ragamuffinonline.co.uk
Displays of vivid hand-made chunky knitwear, scarves and toys catch your eye in the huge windows of this shop, found on the corner of St. Mary's Street.
🖽 G6 ✉ 276 Canongate EH8 8AA ☎ 0131 557 6007 🚍 35

### THE TAPPIT HEN
This tiny shop specializes in traditional Celtic knot-work wedding rings, handmade in precious metals, plus a range of gifts made from pewter.
🖽 F6 ✉ 89 High Street EH1 1SG ☎ 0131 557 1852 🚍 35 and all North Bridge buses

### WILLIAM CADENHEAD
A quaint shop hidden at the bottom of the Royal Mile, specializing in malt whiskies and old oak-matured Demerara rum.
🖽 G6 ✉ 172 Canongate EH8 8BN ☎ 0131 556 5864 🚍 35

### YE OLDE CHRISTMAS SHOPPE
www.scottishchristmas.com
This family-run shop sets a festive scene with its Christmassy red façade, warm atmosphere and hand-crafted festive gifts.
🖽 G6 ✉ 145 Canongate 🍴 H8 8BN ☎ 0131 557 9220 🚍 35

# Entertainment and Nightlife

## BONGO CLUB

www.thebongoclub.co.uk
Popular and chilled hot spot that boasts interesting club nights, covering different genres of music, from funk and house to jazz and rare grooves.
➕ G6 ✉ Moray House, 37 Holyrood Road EH8 8AQ ☎ 0131 558 7604 🕐 Daily 10pm–3am (but times can vary) 🚌 35

## BRASS RUBBING CENTRE

www.cac.org.uk
Great choice of brasses—medieval knights, Pictish symbols and Celtic designs. No experience needed and staff are on hand to help. Equipment is provided.
➕ F6 ✉ Trinity Apse, Chalmers Close, High Street EH1 1SS ☎ 0131 556 4364 🕐 Apr–end Sep Mon–Sat 10–5; also Aug Sun 12–5 🚌 35 and all North Bridge buses 🦽 None 🖐 Free, small charge for rubbing

## SCOTTISH STORY-TELLING CENTRE

www.scottishstorytelling centre.co.uk
Refurbished to provide more capacity for its Scottish and children's plays, and story and poetry readings.
➕ F6 ✉ 43–45 High Street EH1 1SR ☎ 0131 556 9579 🕐 Mon–Sat 10–6, Sun (Jul–Sep only) 12–6 ☎ 0131 556 9579 🚌 35 and all North Bridge buses 🦽 Good 🖐 Free

## THE TASS

Named after Rabbie Burns' song The Silver Tassle, you can find live performances of traditional Celtic music on most nights here. Good food and beer.
➕ F6 ✉ Corner of High Street and St. Mary's Corner EH1 1SR ☎ 0131 556 6338 🚌 35 and all North Bridge buses

# Restaurants

## PRICES

Prices are approximate, based on a 3-course meal for one person.
£££ over £25
££ £15–£25
£ under £15

## DUBH PRAIS RESTAURANT (££)

www.dubhpraisrestaurant.com
Truly Scottish fare with the very best haggis, beef, lamb, venison and mouthwatering salmon.
➕ F6 ✉ 123b High Street EH1 1SG ☎ 0131 557 5732 🕐 Dinner Tue–Sat 🚌 23, 27, 35, 41, 42, 45

## OFF THE WALL (£££)

www.off-the-wall.co.uk
An uncomplicated modern approach to cuisine leaves the perfectly

### VEGETARIAN

David Bann ensures quality and attention to detail at his well-designed bar/restaurant. Clean, rich tones, natural wood and soft lighting set the mood for modern vegetarian and vegan cuisine. Vegetarianism has never been this cool before.
✉ F6 ✉ 56–58 St. Mary's Street EH1 1SX ☎ 0131 556 5888; www.davidbann.co.uk

prepared food to speak for itself—with the odd surprise, such as squab pigeon with black pudding and orange sauce.
➕ F6 ✉ 105 High Street, Royal Mile EH1 1SG ☎ 0131 558 1497 🕐 Lunch, dinner; closed Sun 🚌 23, 27, 35

## PANCHO VILLAS (££)

www.panchovillas.co.uk
Fresh, authentic Mexican dishes with a modern twist can be found at Mayra Munez's excellent restaurant.
➕ G6 ✉ 240 Canongate EH9 8AB ☎ 0131 557 4416 🕐 Lunch, dinner; closed lunch Sun 🚌 35

# New Town

New Town displays Edinburgh's elegant face. The broad Georgian streets are lined with gracious houses with large windows and attractive doorways. Here, too, are the best shopping and eating opportunities.

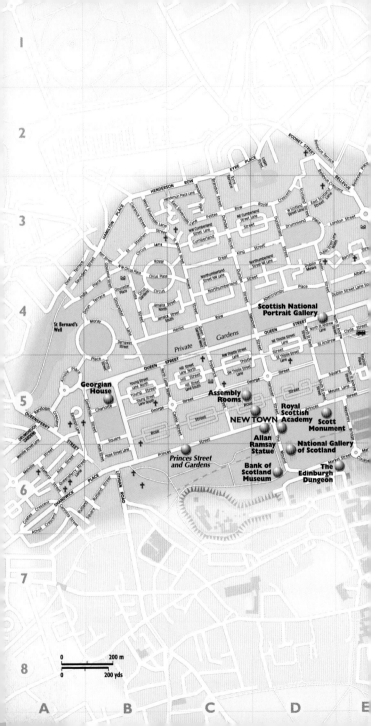

1

2

3

RODNEY STREET
EYRE PLACE
BELLEVUE

HENDERSON ROW

HAMILTON PLACE

Fettes Row
Royal Crescent
W Scotland Street Lane
East Scotland Street Lane
Drummond Place
London Street
Dublin Mews
Albany
Dublin Street Lane South

Circus Place

Circus

Northumberland Place
Abercromby Place

4

St Bernard's Well

Private Gardens

**Scottish National Portrait Gallery**

QUEEN STREET

North St Andrew Lane
Clyde Street

St Andrew

5

**NEW TOWN**

**Georgian House**

QUEEN STREET

**Assembly Rooms**

**Royal Scottish Academy**

Square
Meuse Lane
St Andrew

**Scott Monument**

GEORGE STREET

QUEENSFERRY

DREUMSHEUGH GARDENS

**Allan Ramsay Statue**

**National Gallery of Scotland**

6

CHARLOTTE SQUARE

Princes Street

LOTHIAN ROAD

*Princes Street and Gardens*

**Bank of Scotland Museum**

**The Edinburgh Dungeon**

Market Street

7

8

0        200 m
0        200 yds

A        B        C        D        E

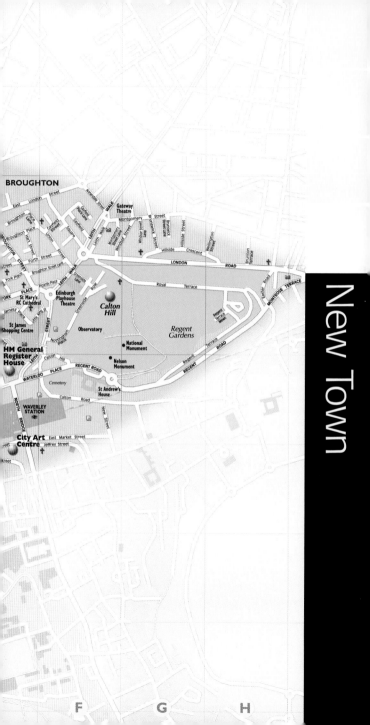

**BROUGHTON**

East London Street
Broughton
Broughton Place
BROUGHTON STREET
Annandale Street
Canfield Street
Hopetoun Street
Albany Street
LEITH WALK
Street
Forth Street
Union Street
Broughton Street Lane

**Gateway Theatre**

Montgomery Street
Brunswick Street
Wellington Street
Hillside Street

Montgomery Street Lane
Windsor Street
Windsor Street Lane

Hillside Crescent
Brunton Terrace

**LONDON ROAD**

Royal Terrace
Montrose Terrace

YORK PLACE
St Mary's RC Cathedral
James's Place
**St James Shopping Centre**
Picardy Place
Little King St

Regent Terrace
Easter Road
Regent Terrace Mews
MONTROSE TERRACE

**Edinburgh Playhouse Theatre**
Greenside Row

**Calton Hill**

**Observatory**

**Regent Gardens**

**HM General Register House**
Calton Hill
**WATERLOO PLACE**
**REGENT ROAD**

**National Monument**

**Nelson Monument**

REGENT ROAD
Regent Road

Cemetery
Calton Road

**St Andrew's House**

**WAVERLEY STATION**
NORTH BRIDGE

New Street

**City Art Centre**
East Market Street
Jeffrey Street

Street

F    G    H

New Town

# Calton Hill

*Edinburgh or Athens? The remarkable Classical buildings of Calton Hill*

## THE BASICS

➕ F4

🚌 X26

🚆 Edinburgh Waverley

ℹ️ Edinburgh and Scotland Information Centre, 3 Princes Street EH2 2QP

☎ 0845 225 5121

### HIGHLIGHTS

● Spectacular views
● Nelson Monument
● National Monument
● City Observatory
● Playfair Monument

**Remarkable buildings grace the top of this volcanic hill, and it is also worth the climb for superb views over the city—Robert Louis Stevenson's most-loved vista of Edinburgh.**

**Grandiose style** Calton Hill (108m/354ft) was known as the Athens of the North in 18th-century Edinburgh. This reputation reached almost absurd proportions when a reproduction of the Parthenon was planned, as a memorial to the Scots killed in the Napoleonic Wars. Work began in 1822, but it is said that the money ran out in 1829 and, with only 12 columns completed, the prolific Edinburgh architect William Playfair's grandiose monument became known as 'Edinburgh's Disgrace'. The remaining folly, however, is part of the distinctive skyline of Calton Hill.

**Other monuments** Sharing the slopes of Calton Hill with the National Monument are the Old Observatory (the only surviving building by New Town planner James Craig) and the City Observatory built in 1818, which has exhibitions and viewings of the night sky. Also on the hill is the 1816 tower of the Nelson Monument, a 143-step climb, but worth the effort for a wider view. The climb to the windy park at the top is rewarded by superb views. Here on the grassy slopes you can see south to the red-toned cliffs of Salisbury Crags and down to undulating slopes of Holyrood Park or to the east beyond Princes Street. Despite its grand Classical structures, Calton Hill is still very much revered as common ground to many locals.

*Robert Adam's Georgian House (right) has some classic 18th-century displays (left)*

# Georgian House

This elegant house, with its preserved period interiors, gives you the chance to glimpse into the lives of the prosperous classes who lived in the New Town in the 18th century.

**How the other half lived** The north side of Charlotte Square is the epitome of 18th-century New Town elegance and was designed by architect Robert Adam (1728–92) as a single, palace-fronted block. With its symmetrical stonework, rusticated base and ornamented upper levels, it is an outstanding example of the style. The Georgian House, a preserved residence on the north side of the square, oozes gracious living. It is a meticulous re-creation by the National Trust for Scotland, reflecting all the fashionable details of the day, right down to the Wedgwood dinner service on the dining table and the magnificent drawing room with its beautiful candlesticks.

**Georgian elegance** The 18th-century monied classes knew what they wanted. As you step in the door of this house you can't help but be impressed by the balustraded staircase and its stunning cupola above, flooding the building with light. The stairs lead to the first floor and the Grand Drawing Room, perfect for entertaining.

**Below stairs** For a contrast, take a look in the basement at the kitchen and the well-scrubbed areas, including the wine cellar and china closet. Here the hard work took place, reflecting the marked social divides of the time.

## THE BASICS

www.nts.org.uk

➕ B5

✉ 7 Charlotte Square EH2 4DR

☎ 0131 226 3318

🕐 Apr–end Oct daily 10–5 (Jul–Aug 10–7); Mar, Nov–end Dec daily 11–3

🚌 13, 19, 36, 37, 41

🚉 Edinburgh Waverley

♿ Limited; six steps to ground floor

✋ Moderate

### HIGHLIGHTS

● Staircase and cupola
● Grand Drawing Room
● Dining Room
● Basement with kitchen

NEW TOWN

★

TOP 25

# National Gallery of Scotland

## HIGHLIGHTS

● *The Revd Dr Robert Walker Skating on Duddingston Loch* by Sir Henry Raeburn
● Monet's *Haystacks*
● Botticelli's *The Virgin Adoring the Sleeping Christ Child*
● Land- and seascapes by William McTaggart
● Works by Old Masters including Vermeer, Van Dyck, Raphael and Titian

**This striking mid-19th-century Classical revival building houses superb Old Masters and an outstanding Scottish collection. It is the perfect setting for Scotland's finest art.**

**Artistic venue** The gallery was designed by New Town architect William Playfair (1789–1857) and completed in the year of his death. It is easily spotted thanks to the huge golden stone pillars of its neoclassical flanks and should not be confused with the nearby Royal Scottish Academy, which has been refurbished as an international exhibition venue (▷ 76).

**What's on show** The gallery's collection of paintings, sculptures and drawings runs to more than 20,000 items, displayed in intimate and accessible

*Clockwise from far left: Botticelli's* Virgin Adoring the Sleeping Christ Child, *c1490 Busts adorn the gallery stairs; the pretty sculpture is in direct contrast to Benjamin West's* Death of the Stag, *1786; Monet's* Haystacks: Snow Effect, *1891; Raeburn's* Revd Dr Robert Walker Skating, *c1795; the grandiose façade of the gallery*

surroundings. At its heart are paintings by the great masters of Europe, including Vermeer, Frans Hals, Tiepolo, Van Dyck, Raphael and Titian. Look out for Monet's *Haystacks* (1891), Velázquez's *Old Woman Cooking Eggs* (1618) and Botticelli's masterpiece *Virgin Adoring the Sleeping Christ Child* (c1490). A fabulous collection of paintings by English landscape artist J. M. W. Turner (1775–1851) is displayed in January each year.

**Scottish contingent** Not surprisingly, the gallery has an outstanding collection of works by Scottish artists. Preferences here include Raeburn's unusual 1795 portrait of *The Revd Dr Robert Walker Skating*, and the sweeping land- and seascapes of William McTaggart. Look out for the vivid scenes of everyday life among the common people, as captured on canvas by Sir David Wilkie.

**THE BASICS**

www.nationalgalleries.org
✚ D6
✉ The Mound EH2 2EL
☎ 0131 624 6200
🕐 Daily 10–5, Thu until 7pm
🍴 Café
🚌 3, 10, 17, 23, 24, 27, 44 and others; a free bus links all five national galleries
🚉 Edinburgh Waverley
♿ Very good
🎟 Free
❓ Shop stocks cards, books and gifts

71

# New Town

## HIGHLIGHTS

● Charlotte Square
● The Georgian House
(▷ 69)
● The Mound

**A product of the lack of space in Edinburgh's Old Town, this spectacular piece of Georgian town planning was instigated by a competition in 1766 to build a fine 'New Town'.**

**Georgian streets** Edinburgh's so-called New Town covers an area of about 318ha (1sq mile) to the north of Princes Street, and is characterized by broad streets of spacious terraced houses with large windows and ornamental door arches. The original area comprised three residential boulevards to run parallel with the Old Town ridge: Princes Street, George Street and Queen Street. With a square at each end (St. Andrew and Charlotte), they were also linked by smaller roads—Rose Street and Thistle Street—to shops and other commercial services. While Princes Street has lost its shine

*The entrance to this 18th-century house in New Town looks a picture with its floral display (left); created from a huge pile of rubbish, the Mound went on to support Edinburgh's most prestigious art galleries (middle); details of the Georgian ideal, with typical fanlight and porch, and ornate lamp outside (right)*

through commercial activity, wide Charlotte Square, with its preserved Georgian House (▷ 69), is the epitome of the planners' intentions.

**Other highlights** It took 2 million cartloads of rubble to create the Mound, later home to the National Gallery (▷ 70–71) and the Royal Scottish Academy (▷ 76). The Mound came about by accident, when 'Geordie' Boyd, a clothier in the Old Town, started to dump rubble in the marsh. Soon the builders from the New Town joined in as they dug out foundations for the new buildings. Another highlight of New Town is Stockbridge, a former mining village developed as part of the second New Town. It was on land owned by the painter Sir Henry Raeburn and went on to become a Bohemian artisans' corner. Ann Street is now one of the city's most exclusive addresses.

**THE BASICS**

➕ D5

ℹ Edinburgh and Scotland Information Centre, 3 Princes Street EH2 2QP ☎ 0845 225 5121

🚉 Edinburgh Waverley

# Princes Street and Gardens

Edinburgh's most famous street at dusk (left); Ross fountain in the gardens (right)

## THE BASICS

+ C5/C6
✉ Princes Street
🕐 Gardens: 7am–10pm summer, 7–5 winter
🚉 Edinburgh Waverley
✋ Free

## HIGHLIGHTS

● Great views to the castle
● Jenner's department store –the world's oldest (▷ 79)
● Floral clock
● Summer band concerts

**Originally designed as a residential area, the most famous street in Scotland is now where local people come to shop. The gardens are a welcome escape from the urban buzz.**

**Changes over time** If you stroll along Queen Street today, you can see how it echoes Princes Street and gives an insight to James Craig's original residential plan. He designated today's Thistle and Rose streets, lesser byways between the grand thoroughfares, as the living and business place of tradespeople and shopkeepers. The use of the lanes behind Thistle and Rose streets to reach the back doors of the wealthier residents was a clever element in his deceptively simple scheme. By the mid-19th century developments began to encroach from east to west. The gracious Georgian buildings began to deteriorate, some replaced by grim, practical edifices in the 20th century.

**Getting its name** Princes Street was originally to be called St. Giles Street, but King George III objected as it reminded him of the St. Giles district of London, which was notorious for its lowlife. This famous street became Prince's Street after the Prince Regent, assuming its plural form in 1848.

**Oasis of green** Princes Street Gardens are a pleasant place to sit down and admire the backs of the Old Town tenements across the valley. In summer there are band concerts to enjoy, and an Edinburgh institution since 1902, the floral clock—a flowerbed planted up as a clock.

# More to See

## ALLAN RAMSAY STATUE
In the West Princes Street Gardens is a statue of the former wig-maker turned poet, Allan Ramsay (1684–1758). The statue is by Sir John Steel (1865).
🕂 D5 ✉ West Princes Street Gardens
🚌 3, 10, 17, 23, 24, 27

## ASSEMBLY ROOMS
www.assemblyroomsedinburgh.co.uk
Even if you're not attending a concert here, it's worth visiting to admire the elegance of the rooms, which opened in 1787, in particular the fine ballroom and huge music hall.
🕂 C5 ✉ 54 George Street EH2 2LR
☎ 0131 220 4348 🕐 Check there is no function 🚌 24, 29, 42 🚉 Edinburgh Waverley
♿ Good 🖐 Varies for performances

## BANK OF SCOTLAND MUSEUM
Located in the bank's headquarters, this small, unusual museum displays old maps, prints, gold coins, bank notes, forgeries and bullion chests.
🕂 D6 ✉ Bank of Scotland Head Office, The Mound, Edinburgh EH1 1YZ ☎ 0131 243 5464 🕐 Tue–Fri 10–5, Sat, Sun 1–5
🚌 23, 27, 41, 42 🚉 Edinburgh Waverley
♿ Good 🖐 Free

## CITY ART CENTRE
www.cac.org.uk
Established in 1980, the gallery is housed in a six-floor former warehouse. It stages changing exhibitions and displays the city's collection of Scottish paintings, including works by the 20th-century Scottish Colourists.
🕂 E6 ✉ 2 Market Street EH1 1DE ☎ 0131 529 3993 🕐 Mon–Sat 10–5, Sun 12–5
🚌 3, 3A, 31, 33, 36 🚉 Edinburgh Waverley
♿ Very good 🖐 Free; charge for some exhibitions

## THE EDINBURGH DUNGEON
www.thedungeons.com
Deep beneath the paving stones of Edinburgh encounter witch-hunters, grave-robbers and murderers; expect darkness and special effects. Not for the fainthearted or very young children.
🕂 E6 ✉ 31 Market Street EH1 1QB
☎ 0131 240 1000 🕐 Mid-Mar to end Jun, Sep–end Oct daily 10–5; Jul, Aug daily 10–7; Nov to mid-Mar Mon–Fri 11–4, Sat, Sun

*Georgian grandeur in the Assembly Rooms*

10.30–4.30 🚌 All buses to Waverley Station (one-minute walk) 🚆 Edinburgh Waverley 🏢 Phone for details 💷 Expensive

## HM GENERAL REGISTER HOUSE
www.nas.gov.uk

Register House was originally sited in the castle and then in the Tolbooth. In 1774 a custom-built Register House in Princes Street was designed by Robert Adam to house the national archives. Still in use today, it is guarded by a famous statue of Wellington.

➕ E5 ✉ Scottish Record Office, 2 Princes Street EH1 3YT ☎ 0131 535 1314 🕐 Mon–Fri 9–4.30 🚆 Edinburgh Waverley 🦽 Good 💷 Free

## ROYAL SCOTTISH ACADEMY
www.royalscottishacademy.org

William Playfair's lovely Classical building has been fully restored and is now linked to the National Gallery to create a superb space for displaying art.

➕ D5 ✉ The Mound EH2 2EL ☎ 0131 225 6671 🕐 Daily 10–5, Thu until 7 🚌 3, 10, 17, 23, 24, 27, 44; free bus linking main galleries 🚆 Edinburgh Waverley

🦽 Very good 💷 Free; charge for some exhibitions

## SCOTT MONUMENT
www.cac.org.uk

Generations have climbed this 61m (200ft) structure since it opened in 1846 to appreciate fine views of the city. Take a closer look at the stone figures, characters from Scott's novels.

➕ D5 ✉ East Princes Street Gardens EH2 2EJ ☎ 0131 529 4068 🕐 Mon–Sat 9–6, Sun 10–6 (closes at 3 Oct–end Mar) 🚆 Edinburgh Waverley 💷 Moderate

## SCOTTISH NATIONAL PORTRAIT GALLERY
www.natgalscot.ac.uk

This gallery tells the history of Scotland through the portraits of the great and the good, the bad, the beautiful and the vain. A host of familiar faces including, of course, Robert Burns.

➕ D4 ✉ 1 Queen Street EH2 1JD ☎ 0131 624 6200 🕐 Daily 10–5, Thu until 7 🚌 8, 10, 12, 16, 23, 27; a free bus links main galleries 🚆 Edinburgh Waverley 🦽 Very good 💷 Free; charge for some exhibitions

*View from the Scott Monument*

*Home to the illustrious, the Scottish National Portrait Gallery*

# Georgian Faça
## of New Town

Explore New Town's streets and squares, full of superb Georgian architecture. For shopping try Princes Street and Multrees Walk.

**DISTANCE:** 4km (2.5 miles)  **ALLOW:** 1 hour 30 minutes, plus stops

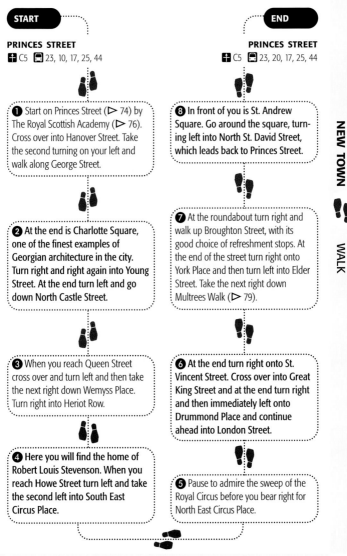

**START**

**PRINCES STREET**
✚ C5  🚌 23, 10, 17, 25, 44

**END**

**PRINCES STREET**
✚ C5  🚌 23, 20, 17, 25, 44

**1** Start on Princes Street (▷ 74) by The Royal Scottish Academy (▷ 76). Cross over into Hanover Street. Take the second turning on your left and walk along George Street.

**2** At the end is Charlotte Square, one of the finest examples of Georgian architecture in the city. Turn right and right again into Young Street. At the end turn left and go down North Castle Street.

**3** When you reach Queen Street cross over and turn left and then take the next right down Wemyss Place. Turn right into Heriot Row.

**4** Here you will find the home of Robert Louis Stevenson. When you reach Howe Street turn left and take the second left into South East Circus Place.

**8** In front of you is St. Andrew Square. Go around the square, turning left into North St. David Street, which leads back to Princes Street.

**7** At the roundabout turn right and walk up Broughton Street, with its good choice of refreshment stops. At the end of the street turn right onto York Place and then turn left into Elder Street. Take the next right down Multrees Walk (▷ 79).

**6** At the end turn right onto St. Vincent Street. Cross over into Great King Street and at the end turn right and then immediately left onto Drummond Place and continue ahead into London Street.

**5** Pause to admire the sweep of the Royal Circus before you bear right for North East Circus Place.

**NEW TOWN**

**WALK**

77

# Shopping

### ADAM ANTIQUES

Large showroom of 18th- and 19th-century furniture—chests, chairs, tables, wardrobes. Restoration work is undertaken.

➕ C4 ✉ 23c Dundas Street EH3 6QQ ☎ 0131 556 7555 🚌 13, 23, 27

### ANTHONY WOODD GALLERY

www.anthonywoodd.com
Traditional art—mainly 19th-century oils, water-colours and prints, from landscapes to caricatures and sporting and military subjects. Also excellent contemporary art.

➕ C4 ✉ 4 Dundas Street EH3 6HZ ☎ 0131 558 9544/5 🚌 13, 23, 27

### BELINDA ROBERTSON

www.belindarobertson.com
Scotland's renowned cashmere designer has come to the heart of Edinburgh's New Town. Belinda's creations, which include sweaters, gloves and scarves as well as cashmere knickers and G-strings, have been donned by the likes of Nicole Kidman and Madonna.

➕ C4 ✉ 13 Dundas Street EH3 6QG ☎ 0131 557 8118 🚌 13, 23, 27

### DICKSON & MACNAUGHTON

www.dicksonandmacnaughton.com
For the archetypal country gentleman (or woman), this established store sells high-quality country clothing by all the leading manufacturers. It also stocks a full range of fishing and shooting accessories.

➕ C5 ✉ 21 Frederick Street EH2 2NE ☎ 0131 225 4218 🚌 24, 29, 42

### FLING

www.fling-scotland.com
Fresh and modern shop using cashmere, leather and silk to produce a range of luxury gifts and accessories. Many items have been designed by owner Deirdre Nicholls.

➕ A6 ✉ 18 William Street EH3 7NH ☎ 0131 226 4114 🚌 4, 12, 25

### FRASERS

www.houseoffraser.co.uk
This popular department store offers a comprehensive selection of clothes (including designer names like DKNY and Ralph Lauren), accessories, perfumes and kitchenware. There is a

---

**DESIGNER FASHION**

Until not so long ago, Glasgow was considered to rule supreme over Edinburgh when it came to shopping for designer names. But now things have changed. Edinburgh is challenging its rival with stylish home-grown boutiques, international fashion outlets and top department stores. A string of designer names have extended their empires to Edinburgh.

---

café on the fifth floor.

➕ D5 ✉ 145 Princes Street EH2 4YZ ☎ 0870 160 7239 🚌 3, 10, 17, 23, 24, 27, 44 and others

### HAMILTON & INCHES

www.hamiltonandinches.com
Established in 1866, the city's most reputable jeweller offers fine imaginative jewellery and silverware. In a grand old building with workshops above and an ornate interior complete with chandeliers.

➕ D5 ✉ 87 George Street EH2 3EY ☎ 0131 225 4898 🚌 13, 23, 24, 27, 29, 42

### HARVEY NICHOLS

www.harveynichols.com
Scotland's first branch of this exclusive London department store added a touch of glamour when it opened in Edinburgh in 2002. Perfumes, designer handbags, accessories and clothes including Gucci, Burberry, Prada, Fendi and Dior. A bar, brasserie and top-floor restaurant add plenty of options for refreshment after hectic shopping.

➕ E4 ✉ 30–34 St. Andrew Square EH2 2AD ☎ 0131 524 8388 🚌 8, 10, 11, 12, 16

### HECTOR RUSSELL

www.hector-russell.com
Part of a well-known chain of kilt shops, this branch allows you to rent, as well as buy. It's all here, from a *sgian dubh* (small knife worn inside the sock) to the complete

outfit. The shop will arrange for your purchases to be mailed home. Additional branch in High Street.

🔲 D5 ✉ 95 Princes Street EH2 2ER ☎ 0131 225 3315; freephone order number (UK only) 0800 980 4010 🚌 3, 10, 17, 25, 44

## HELEN BATEMAN
www.helenbateman.com
For bona fide limited editions designed by the owner, visit this exclusive store that displays a superb range of shoes, boots and accessories that are unique and also affordable.

🔲 A6 ✉ 16 William Street EH3 7NH ☎ 0131 220 4495 🚌 4, 12, 25

## JANE DAVIDSON
www.janedavidson.co.uk
Owner Sarah Davidson has built her reputation on providing excellent service. The three-floor Georgian town house stocks exclusive cashmere labels from around the world and features many top designers, such as Allegra Hicks and Diane Von Furstenberg.

🔲 C5 ✉ 52 Thistle Street EH2 1EN ☎ 0131 225 3280 🚌 23, 27, 29, 42

## JENNERS
www.jenners.com
Edinburgh's grand old dame was founded in 1838 and occupies a magnificent building. The rabbit warren inside, with a central galleried arcade,

houses over 100 departments, from clothes and shoes to perfume, glassware, groceries and toys. There are four cafés. Now owned by House of Fraser.

🔲 E5 ✉ 48 Princes Street Edinburgh EH2 2YJ ☎ 0870 607 2841 🚌 3, 10, 17, 23, 24, 27, 44 and others

## JOSEPH BONNAR
In business since the 1960s, Joseph Bonnar boasts Scotland's largest range of antique jewellery, plus other items.

🔲 C5 ✉ 72 Thistle Street EH2 1EN ☎ 0131 226 2811 🚌 23, 27, 29, 42

## LINZI CRAWFORD
www.linzicrawford.com
The only stockist of

### WALK THE WALK

Multrees Walk—or The Walk as it's known—has provided a new focal point for designer shopping in Edinburgh, creating a stylish pedestrianized shopping street anchored at one corner by the five-floor Harvey Nichols department store. The Walk has attracted a whole host of prestigious international retailers, such as Links of London, Mulberry, Azendi, Calvin Klein, Louis Vuitton and Emporio Armani, with still more to come. The south end of the street leads out onto St. Andrew Square, one of the most prestigious addresses in the city.

several emerging European labels, along with Linzi's own line of merino and cashmere in a distinct shades.

🔲 D4 ✉ 27 Dublin Street EH3 6NL ☎ 0131 558 7558 🚌 13

## MCNAUGHTAN'S BOOKSHOP
www.mcnaughtansbookshop. com
A highly respected second-hand and antiquarian bookshop where casual browsing can sometimes unearth a real gem. The helpful owner, Elizabeth Strong, will search for specific titles.

🔲 F4 ✉ 3a/4a Haddington Place, Leith Walk EH7 4AE ☎ 0131 556 5897 🚌 7, 10, 11, 12, 14, 16, 22, 25, 34, 49

## MOLTON BROWN
www.moltonbrown.co.uk
The simple clean lines of this store are reflected in the products, pampering lotions and delectable fragrances for men and women.

🔲 D5 ✉ 35a George Street EH2 2HN ☎ 0131 225 8452 🚌 13, 19, 37, 41

## NATIONAL GALLERY OF SCOTLAND
www.natgalscot.ac.uk
The Weston Link shop has a wide range of gifts, prints, jewellery, books and postcards. Lots of designs from the gallery's collection, including *The Revd Dr Robert Walker Skating on Duddingston Loch* by

Sir Henry Raeburn.
🔲 D6 ✉ The Mound EH2 2EL ☎ 0131 624 6200 🚌 3, 10, 17, 23, 24, 27, 44; free gallery bus

## PRINCES MALL
www.princesmall-edinburgh.co.uk
Light and spacious shopping mall with more than 40 stores, including high-street outlets and specialty shops. There is a rooftop café and a food court in the lower mall. The mall is next to Waverley train station.
🔲 E5 ✉ Princes Street EH1 1BQ ☎ 0131 557 3759 🚌 3, 23, 22, 25, 27, 29

## RANDOLPH GALLERY
www.randolphgallery.com
Small space with changing exhibitions dealing mainly in realist art from local artists. Dundas Street is the city's main street for contemporary art.
🔲 C4 ✉ 39 Dundas Street EH3 6QQ ☎ 0131 556 0808 🚌 13, 23, 27

## ST. JAMES CENTRE
www.stjamesshopping.com
Modern shopping mall at the east end of Princes Street. With more than 50 high-street names, the main draw here is the John Lewis department store, which boasts a popular café with panoramic views over the city.
🔲 E4 ✉ Leith Street EH1 3SS ☎ 0131 557 0050 🚌 1, 5, 7, 14, 19, 22, 25, 34

## STEWART CHRISTIE & CO.
Bespoke tailors for more than 200 years, Stewart Christie & Co make garments on the premises. This family business provides a range of country and formal clothing, including Scottish tweed jackets and moleskin trousers as well as Highland dress and tartan evening trousers.
🔲 D4 ✉ 63 Queen Street EH2 4NA ☎ 0131 225 6639 🚌 12, 13, 15, 23, 27, 29, 42

## STUDIO ONE
West End shop in a basement setting. This is a popular address for an attractive range of fun and funky gifts, furnishings and household items.
🔲 A6 ✉ 10–16 Stafford Street EH3 7AU ☎ 0131 226 5812 🚌 12, 25, 44

### WILLIAM STREET
This cobbled street in Edinburgh's West End (at the junction of Stafford and Alva streets) has a concentration of small, specialized shops. Many independent designers have set up shop, selling exclusive clothes, accessories and gifts. William Street attracts women who want to indulge themselves, while their men can check out one of the old traditional pubs, which help to retain the original character of the street.

## TISO
www.tiso.com
Helpful staff offer knowledgeable advice on the quality outdoor clothing and equipment they sell here—all you need for walking, climbing, camping or skiing, and there is also a good mountaineering and travel book section.
🔲 C5 ✉ 123–125 Rose Street EH2 3DT ☎ 0131 225 9486 🚌 13, 23, 27, 29

## VALVONA & CROLLA
www.valvonacrolla.co.uk
Much-loved deli that has hardly changed since opening in 1934. Shelves are stacked with the finest Italian produce and wines. Mozzarella is shipped from Naples, an array of cured meats hang from the ceiling, and bread is baked daily.
🔲 F3 ✉ 19 Elm Row EH7 4AA ☎ 0131 556 6066 🚌 7, 10, 11, 12, 14, 16

## WATERSTONE'S
www.waterstones.com
Edinburgh has several branches of this leading bookshop. The one at the west end of Princes Street spreads over several floors, with large windows and a café on the top level that gives great views to the castle. More branches are at the east end of Princes Street, as well as George Street and Ocean Terminal.
🔲 C5 ✉ 128 Princes Street EH2 4AD ☎ 0131 226 2666 🚌 3, 10, 17, 23, 24, 27, 44

# Entertainment and Nightlife

## ASSEMBLY ROOMS
www.assemblyrooms.com
Elegant Georgian building showcasing mainstream Festival Fringe productions, with an impressive ballroom and music hall.
✚ C5 ✉ 50 George Street EH2 2LE ☎ 0131 228 1155 (box office) 🚌 13, 19, 37, 41

## BAILLIE BAR
Sample real ales at this New Town basement pub with an interesting triangular-shape bar and low ceilings.
✚ B3 ✉ 2–4 St. Stephen Street EH3 5AL ☎ 0131 225 4673 🕐 Mon–Thu 11am–midnight, Fri, Sat 11am–1am, Sun 12.30–midnight 🚌 19A, 24, 29, 42

## BLUE MOON CAFÉ
Everybody is welcome at this gay bar, noted for serving the best food in the area all day. Good beers and wines in relaxing surroundings.
✚ E3 ✉ 36 Broughton Street EH1 3SB ☎ 0131 557 0911 🕐 Mon–Fri 11am–12.30am, Sat, Sun 9.30am–12.30am 🚌 8, 17

## CAFÉ ROYAL CIRCLE
Stop by for a drink and admire the ornate ceiling, tiled portraits, stained glass and mahogany carvings, but its huge circular bar takes the stage.
✚ E5 ✉ 19 West Register Street EH2 2AA ☎ 0131 556 1884 🕐 Mon–Wed 11–11, Thu 11am–midnight, Fri, Sat 11am–1am, Sun 12.30–11pm 🚌 3, 10, 17, 23, 24, 27, 44

## CASK AND BARREL
Staff who know their stuff serve the real ales at this conventional pub. If you're not into football don't come on the day of a big match; it's standing room only.
✚ E3 ✉ 115 Broughton Street EH1 3RZ ☎ 0131 556 3132 🕐 Mon–Wed 11am–12.30am, Thu–Sat 11am–1am, Sun noon–12.30am 🚌 8, 17

## CITY NIGHTCLUB
Amazing sports bar and nightclub in the basement of the Scotsman Hotel (entrance in New Town's Market Street), is Edinburgh's most talked about late-night venue.

✚ E6 ✉ 1a Market Street EH1 1DE ☎ 0131 226 9560 🕐 Wed, Fri, Sat to 3am 🚌 3, 5, 7, 30, 31, 33, 37

## EDINBURGH PLAYHOUSE
www.livenation.co.uk
A multi-purpose auditorium that presents big-budget musicals and dance, and concerts featuring leading rock groups. Close to the east end of Princes Street.
✚ F4 ✉ 18–22 Greenside Place EH1 3AA ☎ 0131 524 3333, 0870 606 3424 (ticketmaster 24 hours) 🚌 7, 10, 11, 12, 14, 22, 25, 26, 49

## GRAPE
Chic wine bar with a big selection of wines. The comfy sofas provide an equally good coffee break during the day.
✚ D4 ✉ The Capital Building, 13 St. Andrew Square EH2 2BH ☎ 0131 557 4522 🕐 Mon, Tue, Thu 11am–midnight, Wed 11–11, Fri, Sat 11am–1am, Sun 12.30–11pm 🚌 8, 10, 11, 12, 16

## JAMIE'S SCOTTISH EVENING
www.thistlehotels.com
This delightful dinner show, hosted by the Thistle Hotel, has entertained audiences with Scottish dancing, singing and bagpipes for over 25 years.
✚ F4 ✉ Thistle Hotel, 107 Leith Street EH1 3SW ☎ 0131 556 0111 🕐 Apr–Nov nightly from 7pm 🚌 1, 5, 7, 14, 19, 22, 25, 34

## JONGLEURS

www.jongleurs.com

With over 20 years' experience and a host of well-known comedians passing through its doors, the Edinburgh branch of this chain of comedy clubs is always good for a laugh.

🚇 F4 ✉ Unit 6/7 Omni Centre, Greenside Place EH2 4JN ☎ 0870 787 0707 (for bookings) 🕐 Times vary 🚌 7, 10, 11, 12, 14, 22, 25, 26

## LULU

www.tigerlilyedinburgh.co.uk

Tucked beneath the newest boutique hotel in town, subterranean Lulu is glamorous and just slightly risqué. Underfloor lighting enhances the dancing and twinkling crystals stud the walls.

🚇 B5 ✉ 125 George Street EH2 4JN ☎ 0131 225 5005 🕐 Daily 8pm–3am 🚌 13, 19, 37, 41

## OPAL LOUNGE

The multi-purpose basement space is stylish but casual, and subtly evolves through the day from food to drinking to dancing to funky, soul infused tunes.

🚇 C5 ✉ 51a George Street EH2 2HT ☎ 0131 226 2275 🕐 Daily noon–3am 🚌 13, 23, 24, 27, 29, 42

## RICK'S

www.ricksedinburgh.co.uk

Rick's is a sophisticated cocktail bar, restaurant, breakfast café and boutique hotel all in one.

🚇 C5 ✉ 55a Frederick Street EH2 1LH ☎ 0131 622 7800 🕐 Daily 7am–1am 🚌 24, 29

## ROSS OPEN AIR THEATRE

Impressive spot for a summer schedule of major outdoor concerts and live events, beneath Edinburgh Castle.

🚇 C6 ✉ Princes Street Gardens ☎ 0131 228 8616 🚌 3, 10, 17, 23, 24, 27, 44 and others

## SHANGHAI

www.lemondehotel.co.uk

Located in the basement of a smart boutique hotel, this club is fast gaining the reputation as one of Edinburgh's top clubs and party venues. You can dine and drink in one of the other themed city venues before Shanghai.

🚇 D5 ✉ 16 George Street EH2 2PF ☎ 0131 270 3900 🕐 Daily 9pm–3am 🚌 13, 19, 37, 41

## THE STAND

www.thestand.co.uk

It's easy to forget that not so long ago, once the glut of the Edinburgh Fringe had come and gone, the Scottish comedy scene was a patchy affair. But thanks primarily to the efforts of The Stand Comedy Club a genuine circuit has re-emerged. At this basement bar you can enjoy well-known Scottish comedians and promising new talent, seven nights a week.

🚇 E4 ✉ 5 York Place EH1 3EB ☎ 0131 558 7272 🕐 Mon–Sat 7.30pm–1am, Sat 12.30–midnight 🚌 10, 11, 12, 15, 16, 17, 26, 44

## VUE CINEMA

www.myvue.com

A huge glass-fronted building opposite John Lewis, this multiplex cinema has stadium seating and the latest in digital surround sound. There are 12 screens, three come with Gold Class. The Gold Class ticket gives you luxury leather seats, waiter bar service during the film and a wall-to-wall screen.

🚇 F4 ✉ Omni Centre, Greenside Place EH1 3AA ☎ 0871 224 0240 (box office and information) 🚌 7, 10, 11, 12, 14, 22, 25, 26

# Restaurants

## PRICES

Prices are approximate, based on a 3-course meal for one person.

£££ over £25
££ £15–£25
£ under £15

## ALL BAR ONE (££)

Serving a variety of bistro-style food based on simple recipes, this financial area bolt-hole has a refectory hall theme with large wooden tables.
🔡 D5 ✉ 29–31 George Street EH2 2PA ☎ 0131 226 9971 🕐 Lunch, dinner 🚌 13, 19, 41

## BELLINI (££–£££)

www.bellinirestaurant.co.uk
Italian chef Angelo Cimini prepares secret recipes, some hundreds of years old, that are served in an elegant Georgian dining room. Finest Scottish produce is given a distinctly Italian slant. Also a cooking school.
🔡 D4 ✉ 8b Abercromby Place EH3 6LB ☎ 0131 476 2602 🕐 Dinner only Tue–Sun 🚌 12, 13, 15, 23, 27, 29, 42

## LE CAFÉ ST. HONORÉ (££)

Intimate, relaxed dining in an authentic French-style restaurant. The menu has a fine blend of Scottish and French dishes. Extensive wine list.
🔡 C5 ✉ 34 NW Thistle Street Lane EH2 1EA ☎ 0131 226 2211 🕐 Lunch, dinner; closed Sun 🚌 23, 27, 29, 41

## CIRCUS WINE BAR & GRILL (££)

www.circuswinebarandgrill.co.uk
In new premises from 2007, this is an exciting addition to the Edinburgh café scene. It's the perfect venue whatever the occcasion, with excellent food and a relaxing cocktail bar.
🔡 B5 ✉ 58a North Castle Street EH2 3LU ☎ 0131 226 6743 🕐 Lunch, dinner; closed lunch Sat, Sun 🚌 19, 29, 37

## DOME (£££)

www.thedomeedinburgh.com
Classy venue housed in a converted bank with a magnificent glass dome

## DINE WITH A VIEW

For fine food and spectacular views try the Forth Floor Restaurant at Harvey Nichols (✉ 30–34 St. Andrew Square EH2 2AD ☎ 0131 524 8350), which has a balcony and floor-to-ceiling windows providing striking views of the Castle in one direction and the Firth of Forth in the other. Oloroso (▷ 86) occupies a top-floor corner site with two sides of the building made entirely of glass and an outdoor roof terrace, with stunning views of the castle and across the roof tops to the Firth of Forth. Tower Restaurant (▷ 44) occupies a space above the Museum of Scotland (▷ 27) and offers superb views over Old Town.

as the focal point in the Grill Room bistro. Classic Scottish cuisine surprisingly blended with European and Far East tastes.
🔡 D5 ✉ 14 George Street EH2 2PF ☎ 0131 624 8624 🕐 Lunch, dinner 🚌 29, 42

## DORIC TAVERN (££)

www.thedoric.co.uk
Built in 1710, this bustling bistro has become a meeting place for writers, artists and journalists. Eclectic dishes include venison, steaks and pastas, and sweet potato pie. The downstairs pub serves traditional snacks.
🔡 D6 ✉ 15–16 Market Street EH1 1DE ☎ 0131 225 1084 🕐 Lunch, dinner 🚌 23, 27, 41

## DUCK'S AT LE MARCHÉ NOIR (££)

www.ducks.co.uk
As its name suggests, ducks decorate this cozy restaurant that has soft candlelight and an elegantly restrained ambience. The menu delivers creative combinations of Scottish produce with an international influence. Attentive service.
🔡 C2 ✉ 2 Eyre Place EH3 5EP ☎ 0131 558 1608 🕐 Lunch, dinner; closed lunch Sat, Mon 🚌 23, 27, 36

## EST EST EST (££)

www.estestest.co.uk
Modern Italian cuisine using traditional methods can be found at this stylish restaurant.

Black-and-white photographs adorn the walls and sleek furniture completes the picture. Tasty pizzas from the open fire.

➕ B5 ✉ 135 George Street EH2 4JH ☎ 0870 40 12 109 🕐 Daily lunch, dinner 🚌 13, 19, 37, 41

## LA GARRIGUE (£££)

www.lagarrigue.co.uk
A showcase for food from the Languedoc region in France, the hearty Gallic cooking is presented with finesse and the wines and cheeses are also from the region. With the dominant blue tint and the wooden furniture there is a strong Mediterranean feel.

➕ F6 ✉ 31 Jeffrey Street EH1 1DH ☎ 0131 557 3032 🕐 Lunch, dinner; closed Sun except during festival 🚌 23, 35, 36

## HADRIAN'S BRASSERIE (££)

www.thebalmoralhotel.com
Chic informal brasserie decorated in lime green and a dash of violet, with walnut fittings. Good quality Scottish cuisine with a European influence.

➕ E5 ✉ Balmoral Hotel, 1 Princes Street EH2 2EQ ☎ 0131 557 5000 🕐 Lunch, dinner 🚌 3, 10, 17, 25, 44

## HALDANES (£££)

www.haldanesrestaurant.com
Haldanes continues to maintain its reputation. You will be hard pushed to find refined Scottish country-house cooking to beat this. Dishes such as west coast king scallops, along with Highland venison and Scottish beef are served in the basement dining rooms, furnished with a dash of tartan. Coffee is served with homemade truffles and fudge.

➕ C4 ✉ 13b Dundas Street EH3 3QB ☎ 0131 556 8407 🕐 Dinner; lunch by reservation 🚌 13, 23, 27

## HENDERSON'S SALAD TABLE (£)

www.hendersonsofedinburgh.co.uk
An Edinburgh legend on the vegetarian scene that prides itself on good salads, plus soups, hot dishes and puddings. Lively, cosmopolitan atmosphere, and sometimes live music.

➕ D4 ✉ 94 Hanover Street

---

**EXOTIC TASTES**

While local dishes are still prominent in most of Scotland, in Edinburgh the choice of cuisines from around the world is endless—from Moroccan and Turkish to Thai and Indian. Some restaurants offer exciting fusions of Indian and European cooking or the very latest innovations from Mumbai (Bombay). Newer international trends include Indonesian, Caribbean, Vietnamese, Hungarian, Russian, Mongolian and Mexican.

---

EH2 1DR ☎ 0131 225 2131 🕐 Lunch, dinner; closed Sun except during Festival 🚌 13, 19, 23, 27, 41, 42, 45

## HOWIES (£)

www.howies.uk.com
In a delightful 200-year-old Georgian building, this chain restaurant offers fresh Scottish produce served with imagination at a good price. There are other branches in the city at Stockbridge, Victoria and Bruntsfield.

➕ E5 ✉ 29 Waterloo Place EH1 3BQ ☎ 0131 556 5766 🕐 Lunch, dinner 🚌 8, 29, 37, 37a,

## IGGS (££)

Convivial restaurant with fine views of Calton Hill. The quality organic Scottish cuisine has a Mediterranean influence; there is a Spanish tapas bar next door. Try poached lobster on truffled leeks with lobster caviar sauce, or, for vegetarians, Spanish Gypsy vegetable stew.

➕ F6 ✉ 15 Jeffrey Street EH1 1DR ☎ 0131 557 8184 🕐 Lunch, dinner; closed Sun 🚌 35 and North Bridge buses

## KWEILIN (££)

www.kweilin.co.uk
Enjoy beautifully cooked traditional Cantonese cuisine in plush surroundings. The menu offers a great selection and there is an excellent wine list.

➕ C4 ✉ 19–21 Dundas Street EH3 6QG ☎ 0131 557 1875 🕐 Lunch, dinner;

closed Mon and Sun lunch
📅 23, 27

### THE LIVING ROOM (£–££)

www.thelivingroom.co.uk
Dine or drink among lots of wood, brown leather, murals and pot plants. Good robust stylish food—home-cooking with an international taste. Jazz music on most nights (not Monday).
✚ C5 ✉ 113–115 George Street EH2 4JN ☎ 0870 442 2718 🕐 Daily lunch, dinner
📅 13, 19, 37, 41

### MELROSE RESTAURANT (££)

www.macdonaldhotels.co.uk/roxburghe
The Melrose at the Macdonald Roxburghe Hotel has exciting creations such as loin of lamb with garlic and olive oil mash, honey-glazed veg and beetroot sweet-and-sour jus, served alongside traditional Scottish dishes.
✚ B5 ✉ Macdonald Roxburghe Hotel, 38 Charlotte Square EH2 4HG ☎ 0870 194 2108 🕐 Lunch, dinner; closed Sat and Sun lunch
📅 13, 19, 36, 37, 37A, 41

### MUSSEL INN (££)

www.mussel-inn.com
The tastiest shellfish, scallops and oysters are delivered fresh from the Scottish sea lochs to this bustling eatery in the heart of New Town.
✚ C5 ✉ 61–65 Rose Street EH2 2NH ☎ 0131 225 5979

🕐 Lunch, dinner 📅 3, 12, 29, 44

### NUMBER ONE (£££)

www.thebalmoralhotel.com
Chef Jeff Bland serves luxurious simple dishes created from top-quality ingredients at this classy restaurant. The menu has a range of meats and seafood (braised oxtail, Barbary duck, organic salmon).
✚ E5 ✉ Balmoral Hotel, 1 Princes Street EH2 2EQ
☎ 0131 557 6727 🕐 Dinner only 📅 3, 10, 17 25, 44

### OLIVE BRANCH (££)

www.theolivebranchscotland.co.uk
A trendy mix of black leather, wicker and velour seating in neutral shades against wooden floors and bare brick walls. Large windows enable serious people-watching in an area that is popular for the wild and bold.
✚ E3 ✉ 91 Broughton Street EH1 3RX ☎ 0131 557 8589
🕐 Lunch, dinner 📅 8, 17

### OLOROSO (£££)

www.oloroso.co.uk
An architectural gem, with

### EATING ITALIAN

**Large numbers of Italians emigrated to Scotland in the early 20th century, bringing with them their own culinary influences. Hence, you will find many good Italian restaurants, mostly in Edinburgh's West End.**

floor-to-ceiling glass walls offering panoramic views. Innovative dishes have an Asian influence, such as seared sea bass with butternut squash puree, and chicory and white bean sauce. Have a drink on the terrace for a great view of the castle.
✚ C5 ✉ 33 Castle Street EH2 3DN ☎ 0131 226 7614
🕐 Lunch, dinner 📅 19, 37, 41

### LA P'TITE FOLIE (££)

www.laptitefolie.co.uk
The French cuisine more than measures up to the outstanding Tudor building housing this cheerful eatery, where the tables are rather close together. There is a second branch at 61 Frederick Street.
✚ A5 ✉ Tudor House, 9 Randolph Place EH3 7TE
☎ 0131 225 8678 🕐 Lunch, dinner 📅 13, 19, 36, 37, 41

### VINCAFFÈ (££)

www.valvonacrolla.co.uk
The owners of Scotland's oldest delicatessen, Valvona & Crolla (▷ 80), opened this café/wine bar in 2004, creating a Continental-style meeting place. Their own finest ingredients are used to provide simple or sophisticated Italian food, washed down by a glass of wine from their range.
✚ E4 ✉ 11 Multrees Walk EH1 3DQ ☎ 0131 557 0088
🕐 Lunch, dinner; closed dinner Sun 📅 8, 10, 11, 12, 16

There's plenty to see right on the doorstep of the city and the transport is good. From award-winning Edinburgh Zoo to the Royal Yacht *Britannia* at Leith, the attractions are well worth a visit.

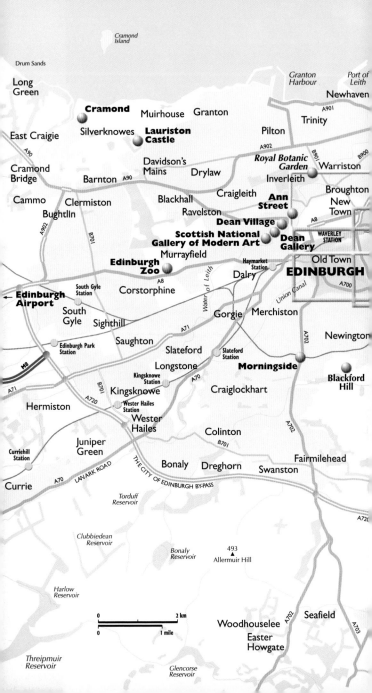

Cramond Island

Drum Sands

Long
Green

Granton
Harbour

Port of
Leith

Newhaven

**Cramond**    Muirhouse    Granton

East Craigie    Silverknowes    **Lauriston Castle**

Trinity

A901

Pilton

Cramond
Bridge

Barnton    A90

Davidson's
Mains

Drylaw

A902

*Royal Botanic Garden*

Inverleith

B901

Warriston

B900

Cammo

Clermiston

Blackhall

Craigleith

Broughton

Bughtlin

Ravelston

**Ann Street**

New
Town

B701

**Dean Village**

A8

**Scottish National Gallery of Modern Art**

**Dean Gallery**

**WAVERLEY STATION**

A902

**Edinburgh Zoo**

Murrayfield

Haymarket
Station

**Old Town**

**EDINBURGH**

← **Edinburgh Airport**

South Gyle
Station

Corstorphine

A8

Dalry

Union Canal

A700

South
Gyle

Sighthill

A71

Gorgie

Merchiston

A702

Newington

Edinburgh Park
Station

Saughton

Slateford

Slateford
Station

**Morningside**

Blackford
Hill

M8

Kingsknowe
Station

Longstone

A70

A71

B701

Kingsknowe

Craiglockhart

Hermiston

A720

Wester Hailes
Station

**Wester Hailes**

A702

Currichill
Station

Juniper
Green

Colinton

B701

Fairmilehead

Currie

A70

LANARK ROAD

Bonaly

THE CITY OF EDINBURGH BY-PASS

Dreghorn

Swanston

A720

Torduff
Reservoir

Clubbiedean
Reservoir

Bonaly
Reservoir

493
▲ Allermuir Hill

Harlow
Reservoir

0                    2 km

0            1 mile

Woodhouselee

A702

Seafield

A703

Threipmuir
Reservoir

Easter
Howgate

Glencorse
Reservoir

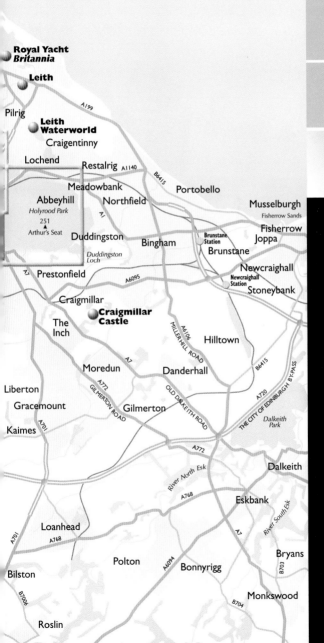

Firth of Forth

**Royal Yacht**
*Britannia*

**Leith**

Pilrig

**Leith Waterworld**

Craigentinny

Lochend

Restalrig A1140

A199

B6415

Meadowbank

Portobello

Abbeyhill

Northfield

Musselburgh

Fisherrow Sands

*Holyrood Park*
251
▲
Arthur's Seat

A1

Duddingston

Bingham

Brunstane Station

Fisherrow
Joppa

Brunstane

*Duddingston Loch*

Newcraighall

Prestonfield

A6095

Newcraighall Station

Stoneybank

Craigmillar

**Craigmillar Castle**

The Inch

MILLER HILL ROAD

A6106

Hilltown

Moredun

A7

Danderhall

B6415

A720

THE CITY OF EDINBURGH BY-PASS

Liberton

A772

GILMERTON ROAD

OLD DALKEITH ROAD

*Dalkeith Park*

Gracemount

Gilmerton

Kaimes

A701

A772

Dalkeith

*River North Esk*

A768

Eskbank

Loanhead

A768

A7

*River South Esk*

B703

A701

Polton

A6094

Bonnyrigg

Bryans

Bilston

B7006

Monkswood

B704

Roslin

# Craigmillar Castle

| HIGHLIGHTS |
|---|

● Views
● Substantial ruins
● Queen Mary's Room
● Former chapel and dovecote

| TIP |
|---|

● Don't be put off by the journey to the castle through some of Edinburgh's less admired housing developments—it's worth the effort.

**The ruins of one of Scotland's most impressive 15th-century tower houses are particularly pleasant to visit when the hustle and bustle of Edinburgh becomes too much.**

**Splendid remains** Craigmillar lies 4km (2.5 miles) southeast of the heart of the city, off the A7, and is often overlooked because of the more famous Edinburgh Castle. At its core is a well-preserved early 15th-century L-plan tower house with walls up to 2.7m (9ft) thick, constructed on the site of an older fortification by Sir George Preston. His grandson, William, added the curtain wall in the 1440s. The main defensive features include massive doors, a spiral turnpike stair (connecting three floors), narrow passageways and two outer walls to fend off English attackers.

*Surprisingly rural considering its proximity to the city, Craigmillar Castle makes a pleasant alternative for an afternoon out*

**Fit for a queen** Mary, Queen of Scots, fled here on several occasions when the pressures of life at Holyrood became too great, notably after the murder of her secretary and darling David Rizzio in 1566, and the tiny chamber where she slept bears her name. It is said that during this stay conspirators agreed to the 'Craigmillar Bond', the plot to kill Lord Darnley, Mary's unscrupulous and unpopular husband.

**Falls into ruin** Craigmillar was bought from the Preston family by Sir John Gilmour in 1660 with the intention to convert it into a fashionable residence. The family, however, decided to move to Inch House at Gilmerton instead and Craigmillar was abandoned. Overgrown and ruinous, it was acquired by the state in 1946. Today it is in the hands of Historic Scotland.

**THE BASICS**

www.historic-scotland.
gov.uk
✚ Off map at M9
✉ Craigmillar Castle Road
EH16 4SY
☎ 0131 661 4445
🕐 Apr–end Sep daily
9.30–5.30; Oct–end Mar
Sat–Wed 9.30–4.30, Thu
9.30–12, Sun 2–4.30
🚍 2, 14
♿ Poor, but access to
visitor area
🎫 Moderate

# Edinburgh Zoo

## HIGHLIGHTS

● Penguin Parade
● Free Hilltop Safari rides
● Rare breeds
● Lion enclosure
● Magic Forest
● Rainy-weather trail
● Conservation trail
● Aerial walkway

### TIP

● Check out the website prior to your visit and download a map and trails so you can plan ahead to make the most out of your time here.

**Long gone are the days of the solitary sad elephant—this fine zoo provides the visitor with an inspirational day out while promoting the conservation of threatened species and habitats.**

**Conservation, education and fun** Located at Corstorphine, 5km (3 miles) west of the heart of the city, Edinburgh Zoo is on the side of a steep hill, covering an area of some 33ha (82 acres). It successfully promotes conservation and education, while demonstrating how a visitor attraction can adapt to survive, allowing close access to around 1,000 animals.

**Natural habitats** The new generation of animal exhibits have brought the crowds back—examples include the aerial walkway across the rolling

*On lookout, a meerkat stands guard at Edinburgh Zoo (far left); checking out the giraffe enclosure (middle); one of the zoo's most popular events, the Penguin Parade, always attracts a big crowd (right); more penguins waddling through the zoo (below left); who's talking to who?—penguin enclosure at Edinburgh Zoo (below right)*

hillocks occupied by the painted hunting dogs, and the African plains. Several other artfully designed enclosures give a sense of spaciousness, including the lion enclosure and the Magic Forest, with its small rainforest monkeys. You can also take a 30-minute free Hilltop Safari ride to the top of the zoo, with commentary on the animals on the way round.

**Penguin parades** The zoo is particularly associated with penguins, with a history of successful breeding. The underwater views of the birds swimming are fascinating. Don't miss the daily stroll outside their enclosure by the penguins at 2.15, from April to September, weather permitting. Overall, a visit to the zoo should be very much a part of the Edinburgh experience, both to see the animals and to enjoy the city views.

**THE BASICS**

www.edinburghzoo.org.uk
✚ Off map at A7
✉ Corstorphine Road EH12 6TS
☎ 0131 334 9171
🕐 Apr–end Sep daily 9–6; Oct, Mar daily 9–5; Nov–end Feb daily 9–4.30
🍴 Restaurant, café, kiosks and picnic areas
🚌 12, 26, 31
♿ Very good
💷 Expensive

# Leith

## HIGHLIGHTS

● The Shore
● Bars and restaurants
● Water of Leith Visitor Centre
● Royal Yacht *Britannia*

## TIP

● Choose a dry and, if possible, sunny day to visit Leith to get the most from the coastal location.

**Edinburgh's seaport, amalgamated with the city in 1921, has been a dock area since the 14th century. Following a decline in shipbuilding, it has been regenerated into a trendy tourist area.**

**New role** Leith was for many years a prosperous town in its own right. As the shipbuilding industry began to wane in the 20th century the town went into decline, but in recent years it has come up in the world, and now it buzzes with fashionable eating places. The area known as The Shore, along the waterfront, has been well restored and is filled with flourishing bars and restaurants. Warehouses, once full of wine and whisky, have been converted into smart accommodation. Where Tower Street meets The Shore, look for the Signal Tower, built in 1686 as a windmill. Edinburgh's river, the Water of Leith,

*Take a cruise out from the waterside at Leith (left); the Waterfront Wine Bar in Leith is in a former lock-keeper's cottage (right); new flats at Leith are becoming popular, especially with young city workers (below left); working boats in Leith docks (below right)*

flows through the middle of the town and the visitor area tells more about its wildlife and heritage.

**Historic Leith** The town has witnessed its share of history—Mary, Queen of Scots, landed here from France in 1561 and stayed at Lamb House, in Water Street. James II of Scotland banned golf from Leith links as it interfered with the army's archery practice. The original 13 rules of golf were drawn up here in 1744, but in 1907 the dunes were flattened to create a public park and golf was banned once more.

**Modern development** For visitors, the Royal Yacht *Britannia* (▷ 97) is the draw, and to access the ship you enter through the Ocean Terminal complex (▷ 104), one of Europe's largest shopping and leisure complexes, with a 12-screen cinema.

**THE BASICS**

➕ Off map at H1
✉ Leith
🚌 1, 11, 16, 22, 34, 35, 36
ℹ Edinburgh and Scotland Information Centre, 3 Princes Street EH2 2QP
☎ 0845 225 5121
**Water of Leith Visitor Centre**
🕐 Daily 10–4
📱 Interactive exhibition inexpensive

# Royal Botanic Garden

**TOP 25**

The entrance gate to the gardens (left) and an orchid from the collection (right)

## THE BASICS

www.rbge.org.uk

🔲 A1

✉ 20A Inverleith Row EH3 5LR

☎ 0131 552 7171

🕐 Apr–end Sep daily 10–7; Mar, Oct daily 10–6; Nov–end Mar daily 10–4

🍴 Terrace Café

🚌 8, 17, 23, 27, also on Majestic Tour route

♿ Good

💷 Moderate charge for the glasshouses; tours moderate

❓ Tours lasting around 90 minutes leave West Gate at 11 and 2, Apr–end Sep. Extensive Botanics gift shop with stationery, plants and related souvenirs

## HIGHLIGHTS

● Rock Garden
● Glasshouse Experience
● Tropical Aquatic House
● Chinese Hillside
● Scottish Heath Garden
● The gates
● Orchid and Cycad House
● Woodland Garden

**Known locally as The Botanics, these gardens boast some 15,500 species, one of the largest collections of living plants in the world. It's possibly Edinburgh's finest recreational asset.**

**City greenery** Occupying this site since 1823, the gardens cover over 28ha (69 acres) of beautifully landscaped and wooded grounds to the north of the city, forming an immaculately maintained green oasis. The garden is walkable from Princes Street via Stockbridge, though you may wish to take the bus back up the hill. It is especially suitable for children as it is dog-free.

**Inside or out?** There are 10 greenhouses to explore, collectively called the Glasshouse Experience and offering a perfect haven on cold days. They include an amazingly tall palm house dating back to 1858, and the Tropical Aquatic House, with its giant waterlilies and an underwater view of fish swimming through the lily roots. Outside, the plants of the Chinese Hillside and the Heath Garden are particularly interesting, and in summer the herbaceous borders are breathtaking. Check out the rhododendron collection and the rock garden, which displays some 5,000 species and is best seen in May. The highest point of the garden has a fine view of the city.

**Striking design** The West Gate, or Carriage Gate, is the main entrance, but don't miss the stunning inner east side gates, designed by local architect Ben Tindall in 1996.

*The Royal Yacht Britannia (left) has a full-size lounge within its hull (right)*

**This former royal yacht is one of the world's most famous ships, now moored in Edinburgh's historic port of Leith. It is 83rd in a long line of royal yachts stretching back to 1660.**

**New role** *Britannia* was decommissioned in 1997 after a cut in government funds. It had carried the Queen and her family on 968 official voyages all over the world since its launch at Clydebank in 1953.

**Vital statistics** For 40 years, *Britannia* served the royal family, sailing more than 1 million miles to become the most famous ship in the world. A compact yacht, it is just 125.6m (412ft) long. It carried a crew of 240, including a Royal Marine band and an additional 45 household staff when the royal family were aboard. The on-shore visitor area sets the scene, telling the history of the ship. A self-guided tour using handsets takes you around the yacht itself. *Britannia* still retains the fittings and furnishings of her working days, which gives an intimate insight into the royals away from usual palace protocol.

**Royal and naval precision** Check out the apartments adorned with hundreds of original items from the royal collection. The grandest room is the State Dining Room, and the most elegant the Drawing Room. Imagine the royal family relaxing in the Sun Lounge and view the modest sleeping quarters. Everything on board is shipshape, from the Engine Room to the fully equipped Sick Bay.

## THE BASICS

www.royalyachtbritannia.co.uk

➕ Off map at H1

✉ Ocean Terminal, Leith EH6 6JJ

☎ 0131 555 5566

🕐 Apr–end Oct daily 9.30–6 (last admission 4.30); Nov–end Mar daily 10–5 (last admission 3.30)

🍴 Cafés and restaurants in Ocean Terminal

🚌 1, 11, 22, 34, 35, 36 and Majestic tour route

♿ Excellent

💷 Expensive

❓ Reservations strongly advised in high season

## HIGHLIGHTS

- Royal Apartments
- Drawing Room
- State Dining Room
- Sun Lounge
- Royal Bedrooms
- Sick Bay and Operating Theatre
- Engine Room
- The Bridge

# Scottish National Gallery of Modern Art

*Bronze running man and* The Blue Fan, *c1922 by F. C. B. Cadell, RSA, RSW*

## THE BASICS

www.nationalgalleries.org

➕ Off map at A5

✉ 75 Belford Road
EH4 3DR

☎ 0131 624 6200

🕐 Daily 10–5

🍴 Gallery Café

🚌 13; free bus links all five national galleries

🚉 Edinburgh Haymarket

♿ Very good

🎟 Free, but may be charges for temporary exhibitions

❓ Shop stocks books, cards, gifts

## HIGHLIGHTS

● Works by the Scottish Colourists, including those by John Duncan Fergusson
● Major works by Picasso, Matisse and Lichtenstein
● Sculptures by Henry Moore and Barbara Hepworth
● Works by contemporary artists, including Damien Hirst and Rachel Whitehead

**The gallery opened at this parkland site in 1984, providing an ideal setting for the work of those who have been in the forefront of modern art: Matisse, Picasso, Hirst, you'll find them all here.**

**Setting the scene** The first thing you see as you arrive at the main gallery is a sweeping, living sculpture of grassy terraces and semicircular ponds, an installation called *Landform UEDA* by Charles Jencks. After such a grand introduction the rest of the gallery seems quite small, but it is certainly large in terms of its enviable and varied collection of modern art from around the world. It is housed in a former school.

**On display** Regularly changing exhibitions occupy the ground floor, with a varied display from the gallery's collection on the first floor. Among these pieces, look out for works by Picasso, Braque and Matisse, Hepworth and Gabo. The work of the early 20th-century group of painters known as the Scottish Colourists is particularly striking, with canvases by Samuel John Peploe (1871–1935), George Leslie Hunter (1877–1931), John Duncan Fergusson (1874–1961) and F. C. B. Cadell (1883–1937). Also of interest are Fergusson's dramatic *Portrait of a Lady in Black* (c1921), the vibrancy of Cadell's *Blue Fan* (c1922) and Peploe's later, more fragmentary work, such as *Iona Landscape, Rocks* (c1927).

**More modern art** Stroll across the road to the Dean Gallery (▷ 99), an outstation of the gallery.

# More to See

## ANN STREET

One of Edinburgh's most exclusive addresses is based on the estate built in 1814 by artist Sir Henry Raeburn in memory of his wife, Ann. Located between Stockbridge and New Town, the houses combine classic splendour with cottagey charm.

🔆 A4 ✉ Ann Street 🚌 29, 37, 41, 42

## BLACKFORD HILL

One of Edinburgh's seven hills, the view from here in all directions is excellent. Just 3km (2 miles) south of central Edinburgh, it is home to the Royal Scottish Observatory, which moved here from Calton Hill in 1895. The visitor area is open only for group visits and occasional events. There are Friday evening viewing sessions in winter that must be booked in advance (☎ 0131 668 8404).

🔆 Off map at D9 ✉ Blackford 🚌 24, 38, 41 ♿ Few

## CRAMOND

There are Roman remains, 16th-century houses, a fine church, an old inn and some elegant Victorian villas to hold your attention in this attractive suburb on the shores of the Firth of Forth. The Cramond Heritage Trust has a permanent exhibition in the Maltings exploring the history of the village. Take one of the good walks around the area or visit Lauriston Castle (▷ 100), nearby.

🔆 Off map at A1 ✉ Cramond
🕐 Maltings: Jun–end Sep Sat, Sun 2–5; every afternoon during Festival 🚌 24, 41

## DEAN GALLERY

www.natgalscot.ac.uk
Across the road from the Scottish National Gallery of Modern Art (▷ 98), this gallery is housed in a former orphanage and displays an excellent collection based around the work of Dada and the Surrealists, and the Scottish sculptor Eduardo Paolozzi (b1924).

🔆 Off map at A5 ✉ 73 Belford Road EH4 13DS ☎ 0131 624 6200 🕐 Daily 10–5
🚌 13; free bus linking main galleries
🚂 Edinburgh Haymarket ♿ Very good
🍴 Free

*Take in the view over Edinburgh from Blackford Hill*

*Rows of boats at Cramond waterside*

## DEAN VILLAGE

The northern limit of New Town is marked by Thomas Telford's 1832 Dean Bridge. It spans a steep gorge created by the Water of Leith. After a decline in grain trade, the workers' cottages, warehouses and mill buildings have been restored and Dean has become a desirable residential area. The cemetery is the resting place of many well-known locals, including the New Town architect William Playfair.

➕ Off map at A5 ✉ Dean 🚌 13, 37, 41

## LAURISTON CASTLE

This 'castle' is the epitome of Edwardian comfort and style, a gabled and turreted mansion in a leafy setting overlooking the Firth of Forth near Cramond. Starting out as a simple tower house, Lauriston was renovated and extended several times. The castle was left to the City of Edinburgh in 1926 by William Robert Reid.

➕ Off map at A1 ✉ 2A Cramond Road South, Davidson's Mains EH4 5QD ☎ 0131 336 2060 🕐 Apr–end Oct Sat–Thu tours at 11, 12, 2, 3, 4; Nov–end Mar Sat, Sun at 12, 2, 3. Grounds open 9am–dusk 🚌 24 ♿ Good 💷 Castle: moderate. Grounds: free

## LEITH WATERWORLD

Fun with a splash. Leisure pool, flumes, slides and water features including wave machine, river run, geysers and more. Also a learner pool. Children under eight must be accompanied by an adult.

➕ Off map at H1 ✉ 377 Easter Road EH6 8HU ☎ 0131 555 6000 🕐 Christmas, Easter and summer (Jul to mid-Aug) school holidays daily 10.30–4.45; Fri–Sun 10.30–4.45 outside holidays 🚌 1, 35 ♿ Good 💷 Moderate

## MORNINGSIDE

Immortalized in the accent of novelist Muriel Spark's Jean Brodie, this southwest suburb still houses the wealthy of the city. A quiet leafy spot graced with Victorian villas, it still oozes gentility. Stroll round its pleasant streets for civilized shopping and afternoon tea.

➕ Off map at B9 ✉ Morningside 🚌 5, 11, 15, 15A, 16, 17, 23, 41

*Buildings at Dean village, on the banks of the Water of Leith*

# Excursions

## MURRAYFIELD

**Developed around the 18th-century Murrayfield House, this western suburb is a pleasant district and popular with city commuters.**

Scottish rugby has made its home here and the stadium hosts games during the Six Nations championships. The stadium was built by the Scottish Football Union and opened in 1925. It has a seating capacity of 67,500. Redevelopment gave Murrayfield a new look and the ground was opened by the Princess Royal in 1994 at a cost of £37 million. Murrayfield still holds the world record for the largest attendance at a rugby game. This was for the match when Scotland played Wales in 1975, drawing an enormous crowd of just over 104,000, packed into the stands.

### THE BASICS

**Distance:** 2km (1.5 miles)
**Journey time:** 20 minutes
**Murrayfield Stadium**,
✉ Corstorphine Road, EH12 5PJ
☎ 0131 346 5000;
www.sru.org.uk
🚹 Good
🚌 12, 22, 26, 31
❓ Stadium tours available

## NORTH BERWICK

**Once a small fishing port, North Berwick, located on the south side of the Firth of Forth to the east of Edinburgh, has developed into a lively holiday resort.**

Pleasure craft crowd the little port and its splendid Victorian and Edwardian architecture suggests prosperity. Golf is a number one attraction of the area dubbed the North Berwick Golf Coast. The sport has been played here since the 17th century. The Scottish Seabird Centre uses the latest technology to take pictures of seabirds nesting on the nearby cliffs and islands, and there are interactive and multimedia displays to interest all the family. Behind the town is the cone of the North Berwick Law, a 187m (613ft) high volcanic plug, with fine views from the top, with an arch made from a pair of whale's jaw bones.

### THE BASICS

**Distance:** 40km (25 miles)
**Journey time:** 30 minutes
🚆 From Waverley
ℹ Quality Street
☎ 01620 892197
**Scottish Seabird Centre**
✉ The Harbour, North Berwick EH39 4SS
☎ 01620 890202;
www.seabird.org
🕙 Apr–end Oct daily 10–6; Nov–end Mar Mon–Fri 10–5, Sat, Sun 10–5.30 (closes 4.30 in Dec and Jan)
💷 Expensive

## THE BASICS

www.rosslynchapel.org.uk
**Distance:** 11km (7 miles)
**Journey time:** 1 hour
✉ Roslin EH25 9PU
☎ 0131 440 2159
🕐 Mon–Sat 9.30–5, Sun 12–4.45
💷 Expensive
🚌 15A (Lothian bus); 62 (First bus)

## ROSSLYN CHAPEL

**In a tiny mining village south of Edinburgh, this is the most mysterious building in Scotland, perched above Roslin Glen.**

Founded in 1446 by William St. Clair, Third Earl of Orkney, the church was to be a large cruciform structure, but only the choir was completed, along with sections of the east transept walls. It is linked with the Knights Templar and other secretive societies, and is even believed by some to be the hiding place of the Holy Grail. It has found increased fame through its connection with the best-selling novel *The Da Vinci Code* by Dan Brown, with over 4.5 million visitors since 1997. Inside is the finest example of medieval stone-carving in Scotland, if not Britain. The chapel remains a place of worship.

## THE BASICS

**Distance:** 26km (16 miles)
**Journey time:** 1 hour
🚂 From Waverley to Dalmeny station
🚌 X4, 43 (First Buses)
ℹ Forth Bridges Tourist Information Centre, Queensferry Lodge Hotel, St. Margaret's Head, North Queensferry ☎ 01383 417759
**Hopetoun House**
✉ South Queensferry EH30 9SL ☎ 0131 331 2451 🕐 Easter to mid-Sep daily 11–5.30 💷 Expensive. Grounds only: moderate

## SOUTH QUEENSFERRY

**From 1129 until 1964, prior to the opening of the road suspension bridge, a ferry operated across the Firth of Forth from South Queensferry. The older, cantilevered rail bridge built in the late-19th century has become an icon of Scotland.**

Only a short ride outside Edinburgh, this little royal burgh is a great place to come and admire the two Forth bridges on a summer's evening. To the west, Hopetoun House—which can only be reached easily by car—is a spectacular early-18th-century mansion built by William Bruce and William Adam. Home to the Marquis of Linlithgow, it is full of fine paintings, original furniture, tapestries and wonderful elaborate rococco detail. From the grounds there are more great views of the Forth bridges.

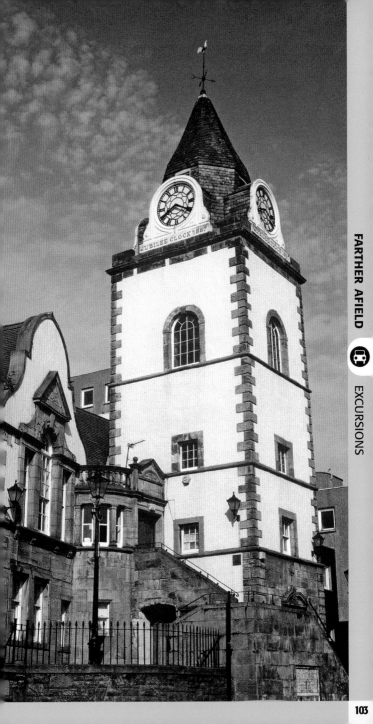

# Shopping

### BAXTERS
www.baxters.com
A large food hall generated from the famous Scottish family, selling all Baxter products and lots more. When you have finished shopping, relax in the restaurant.
🚫 Off map  ✉ Ocean Terminal, Leith EH6 6JJ
☎ 0131 553 0840  🚌 1, 11, 22, 34, 35, 36

### EDINBURGH CRYSTAL VISITOR CENTRE
www.edinburgh-crystal.co.uk
You can buy the eponymous crystal at many shops throughout the city but for a complete experience visit Penicuik, 16km (10 miles) south of the city. You can see how the glass is made, watch master cutters and engravers and browse the shop. There's a seconds shop with up to 70 per cent off.
🚫 Off map  ✉ Penicuik
☎ 01968 675128
🕐 Mon–Sat 10–5, Sun 11–5
🚌 37, 47

### GYLE SHOPPING CENTRE
www.gyleshopping.co.uk
Located to the west of central Edinburgh, this huge retail space of stainless steel and glass has some 60 shops. Easy parking and a food court.
🚫 Off map  ✉ Gyle Avenue, South Gyle Broadway EH12 9JY  ☎ 0131 539 9000
🚌 2, 12, 18, 21, 24, 58

### JAMES PRINGLE WEAVERS
A splendid range of wool items are produced at Leith Mills, including sweaters, tweeds and tartans. Also a vast database of clan ancestry, holding some 50,000 family names.
🚫 Off map  ✉ 70–74 Bangor Road EH6 JJU
☎ 0131 553 5161
🚌 1, 10, 16, 22

### KINLOCH ANDERSON
www.kinlochanderson.com
While browsing for tartan trousers, jackets, kilt outfits, skirts and accessories, you can learn more about the history of tartan from

---

### HAGGIS
Haggis is Scotland's national dish and comes from an ancient recipe for using up the cheapest cuts of meat. It's a sort of large mutton sausage based on the ground-up liver, lungs and heart of a sheep, mixed with oatmeal, onion and spices, and cooked up in the sheep's stomach. It can be dry, greasy or gritty, although when made properly can be delicious—a wee dram of whisky helps wash it down. These days restaurants serve their own spicy versions of the recipe, and if you want a small taster, you'll sometimes find it on the menu as a starter.

---

experts on Highland dress since 1868.
🚫 Off map  ✉ Commercial Street/Dock Street, Leith EH6 6EY  ☎ 0131 555 1390
🚌 16, 22, 25, 36

### LEITH MARKET
The permanent covered market at Leith was first set up in March 2005 and offers a high-quality mix of food, fashion, crafts, antiques, furniture, books and music.
🚫 Off map  ✉ Leith's Commercial Quay  🕐 Sat 9–5.30, Sun 10–4  🚌 22, 35, 36

### OCEAN TERMINAL CENTRE
www.oceanterminal.com
Overlooking the Firth of Forth, this glass-and-steel retail oasis was designed by Jasper Conran and opened in 2001. The complex comes complete with high street names, plus a cinema. Also a venue for exhibitions. Huge free parking area.
🚫 Off map  ✉ Ocean Drive, Leith EH6 6JJ  ☎ 0131 555 8888  🚌 1, 11, 22, 34, 35, 36

### PECKHAMS
www.peckhams.co.uk
Discover the famed MacSween's award-winning haggis, deemed to be the best in Scotland, along with an array of other Scottish specialties. Basement restaurant.
🚫 Off map  ✉ 155–159 Bruntsfield Place EH10 4DG
☎ 0131 229 7054  🚌 11, 15, 16, 17, 23

# Entertainment and Nightlife

## CHURCH HILL THEATRE

Mainly amateur productions but professionals perform here during the Festival.

➕ Off map ✉ 33 Morningside Road EH10 4RR ☎ 0131 447 7597 🚌 5, 11, 15, 16, 17, 23

## DOMINION

www.dominioncinemas.net
This old-fashioned, family-run cinema is the ideal antidote to the multiplex cinemas that are engulfing the city. View latest releases in leather Pullman seats, or indulge in the Gold Class service, which offers leather sofas with complimentary wine or beer and snacks.

➕ Off map ✉ 18 Newbattle Terrace, Morningside EH10 4RT ☎ 0131 447 4771 (box office), 0131 447 2660 (recorded information) 🚌 11, 15, 16, 23

## EDINBURGH CORN EXCHANGE

www.ece.uk.com
Pop and rock venue where acts have included well-known bands such as Blur, Travis and Coldplay.

➕ Off map ✉ 11 Newmarket Road EH14 1RJ ☎ 0131 447 3500 🚌 35 🚆 Slateford from Waverley

## FOOTBALL

Edinburgh's two main professional teams are Heart of Midlothian (Hearts) and Hibernian (Hibs), who play in the Scottish Premier League.

They are at home on alternate Saturday afternoons Aug–May (reserve in advance).

**Hearts FC** ➕ Off map ✉ Tynecastle Stadium, Gorgie Road EH11 2NL ☎ 0131 200 7201; www.heartsfc.co.uk 🚌 3, 3a, 25, 33

**Hibs FC** ➕ Off map ✉ Easter Road Stadium, 12 Albion Place EH7 5QG ☎ 0131 661 1875; www.hibs.co.uk 🚌 1

## HORSE RACING

www.musselburgh-racecourse.co.uk
Musselburgh Racecourse, one of the best small racecourses in Britain, hosts 26 flat and jump meetings a year.

➕ Off map ✉ Linkfield Road, Musselburgh, East Lothian ☎ 0131 665 2859 🚌 15, 15A

## ODEON FORT KINNAIRD

www.odeon.co.uk
A modern complex in a retail park on the outskirts of Edinburgh, with 12

## GOLF

Golf is the national game and with more than 500 courses throughout the country, it's no wonder fanatics flock to the area in pursuit of their first love. The closest courses can be found at Braids Hill, Craigmillar Park and Silverknowes. Visit www.scottishgolf.com for a list of courses and a reservation service.

screens showing a range of mainstream movies.

➕ Off map ✉ 7 Kinnaird Park, Newcraighall Road EH15 3RD ☎ 0871 224 4007 🚌 30; First Bus 141, 142

## OLD DOCK BAR

A pub since 1813, this relaxing traditional bar serves good beer and bistro food and wine. If you want something a bit more cool, try Bar Sirius next door. Both are convenient for Ocean Terminal (▷ 104).

➕ Off map ✉ 3–5 Dock Place, Leith EH6 6LV ☎ 0131 555 4474 🚌 1, 11, 22, 34, 35

## RUGBY

(▷ 101 for Murrayfield information.)

## SWIMMING

Edinburgh is proud of its Olympic-size indoor swimming pool, complete with a diving pool and waterslides.

**Royal Commonwealth Pool** ➕ G9 ✉ 21 Dalkeith Road EH16 5BB ☎ 0131 667 7211 🚌 2, 14, 30, 33

## VUE

www.myvue.com
All the latest releases are shown at this state-of-the-art 12-screen multiplex, with the latest in digital surround sound and comfortable seats that give extra legroom. Free parking.

➕ Off map ✉ Ocean Terminal, Ocean Drive, Leith EH6 6JJ ☎ 0871 224 0240 🚌 1, 11, 22, 34, 35

# Restaurants

### PRICES

Prices are approximate, based on a 3-course meal for one person.

£££ over £25
££ £15–£25
£ under £15

## RESTAURANT AT THE BONHAM (£££)

www.thebonham.com
In a boutique West End hotel (▷ 112), long windows, wooden floors and chic brown-and-cream livery set the scene for stylish contemporary cooking. Desserts such as orange blossom panacotta with lavender tuile are almost too attractive to eat.
➕ Off map ✉ Bonham Hotel, 35 Drumsheugh Gardens EH3 7RN ☎ 0131 623 9319 🕓 Lunch, dinner
🚌 13

## RESTAURANT MARTIN WISHART (£££)

www.martin-wishart.co.uk
Michelin-starred Martin Wishart's brilliantly executed dishes are beautifully presented at this tiny French restaurant on the waterfront at Leith. Bright, modern art stands out against the white walls and stone floors.
➕ Off map ✉ 54 The Shore, Leith EH6 6RA
☎ 0131 553 3557
🕓 Lunch, dinner; closed Sun, Mon, lunch Sat
🚌 16, 22, 35, 36

## RHUBARB (£££)

www.prestonfield.com
James Thompson (of Witchery and Tower restaurant fame) has given this hotel a sumptuous makeover. The food more than matches the opulent setting. High standards mean great food—try the rhubarb crème brûlée. You will need to take a taxi to get here but it's worth the effort.
➕ Off map ✉ Prestonfield Hotel, Priestfield Road EH16 5UT ☎ 0131 225 1333
🕓 Lunch, dinner

## SHIP ON THE SHORE (£££)

Cosy bistro-style bar with a nautical theme. Tasty seafood options may include smoked salmon with lemon, chopped onion and capers and paupiette of sole and

### SCOTTISH SALMON

Scottish salmon is celebrated as being among the best in the world, but beware of the variation between wild (caught) and farmed salmon. Over recent years salmon farming has been hard hit by controversy about fish kept in overcrowded sea cages, the use of dye to tint the flesh and the presence of various chemicals and pollutants. Many salmon farmers have now changed their ways, but many restaurants still consider wild salmon superior.

prawns on braised leeks.
➕ Off map ✉ 24–26 The Shore, Leith EH6 6QN
☎ 0131 555 0409 🕓 Lunch, dinner 🚌 16, 22, 35, 36

## SHORE BAR & RESTAURANT (££)

www.theshore.biz
This informal, zesty establishment in an 18th-century building serves fresh, succulent fish in its wood-panel dining room overlooking the Water of Leith.
➕ Off map ✉ 3 The Shore, Leith EH6 6QW ☎ 0131 553 5080 🕓 Lunch, dinner
🚌 16, 22, 35, 36

## STARBANK INN (££)

www.starbankinn.co.uk
On the waterfront, this inn offers traditional pub food, such as roast lamb with mint sauce, poached salmon, or chicken with tarragon cream sauce, and great views over the Firth of Forth.
➕ Off map ✉ 64 Laverockbank Road, Trinity EH5 3BZ ☎ 0131 552 4141
🕓 Lunch, dinner 🚌 7, 10, 11, 16

## WATERFRONT (££)

www.waterfrontwinebar.co.uk
Pretty quayside restaurant housed in a former lock-keeper's cottage, where fresh, well-prepared fish, meat and vegetarian dishes are served in intimate booths or the vine-clad conservatory.
➕ Off map ✉ 1c Dock Place, Leith EH6 6LU ☎ 0131 554 7427 🕓 Lunch, dinner
🚌 16, 22, 35, 36

Edinburgh has a diverse range of accommodation on offer, from opulent five-star hotels to the lovely, if more humble, Georgian guesthouse. Scottish hospitality is in abundance throughout the city.

Where to Stay

# Introduction

It is important to reserve well in advance if you are considering visiting Edinburgh during Festival time or over Hogmanay for the New Year's celebrations. The quieter times of year will find some bargain deals.

## What the Grades Mean
You may notice that displayed outside all Scottish accommodation is a blue plaque with a thistle symbol. This indicates the star rating issued by VisitScotland (the Scottish Tourist Board). Every type of accommodation is assessed annually and awarded anything from one to five stars to indicate the quality of accommodation, cleanlinesss, ambience, hospitality, service and food and facilities offered.

## En Suite
Bed-and-breakfast accommodation offers the opportunity to stay in somebody's home, and sometimes in some remarkable historical buildings. Be aware that en suite facilities are not always available and bathroom facilities may be shared. If a choice of bath or shower is important to you, check at time of booking.

## Paying
Some hotels will ask for a deposit or full payment in advance, especially for one-night bookings. Some will not take bookings for stays of only one night. Most hotels accept the majority of British and international credit cards, but be aware some smaller guesthouses or B&Bs may not take cards, so check when booking.

Hotels in Edinburgh come in many guises, often in beautiful old buildings

### BED-AND-BREAKFAST
The B&B price generally includes a full cooked breakfast, which in Scotland may consist of any combination of porridge, eggs, fried bread, potato scones, sausage, bacon, mushrooms and tomatoes. Black pudding is often a traditional option, too. Lighter alternatives are usually available. Some establishments offer an evening meal, but you might need to order in advance. While hotels, inns and some guesthouses will have a licence to serve alcohol, few bed-and-breakfasts do.

# Budget Hotels

**PRICES**

Expect to pay under £75 per night for a double room in a budget hotel.

## ABBOTSFORD GUEST HOUSE

www.abbotsfordguesthouse.co.uk

Just north of New Town, this family-run guesthouse has eight individual and well-equipped bedrooms. Breakfast is taken at individual tables in the elegant dining room.

➕ Off map ✉ 36 Pilrig Street EH6 5AL ☎ 0131 554 2706 🚌 11

## BELFORD ROAD HOSTEL

www.edinburghhostels.com

One of several Edinburgh hostels run by the same group. This one is located to the west of New Town in a converted church. Good-quality budget accommodation for students and backpackers, with room for up to 98 guests in dorms, triple, double or family rooms.

➕ Off map ✉ 6–8 Douglas Gardens EH3 3DA ☎ 0131 202 6107; fax 0870 132 5574 🚌 13

## BONNINGTON GUEST HOUSE

www.thebonnington guesthouse.com

The owners extend a warm welcome at this delightful Victorian house not far from Leith, with seven bedrooms finished to a high standard and

retaining original features.

➕ Off map ✉ 202 Ferry Road EH6 4NW ☎ 0131 554 7610 🚌 7, 11, 14

## DENE GUESTHOUSE

www.deneguesthouse.com

Hospitable owners offer a comfortable stay and a good breakfast at this clean and tidy Georgian town house. Well sited in New Town, making it ideal for visiting the city's main sites.

➕ C2 ✉ 7 Eyre Place EH3 5ES ☎ 0131 556 2700; fax 0131 557 9876 🚌 23, 27, 36

## ELMVIEW

www.elmview.co.uk

Part of a stylish Victorian terrace on the edge of Old Town, the three bed-

**SYHA**

The Scottish Youth Hostels Association (SYHA) offers self-catering accommodation hostel-style all over Scotland. In central Edinburgh you can stay at the only 5-star hostel in the city run by the SYHA. Edinburgh Central Hostel is minutes from Waverley Station and Princes Street. It is suitable for individuals, families and groups. There are single, twin and 8-bedded rooms and all are en suite. It has a licensed bistro and self-catering facilities are also available. It's an inexpensive way to be in the heart of the city (✉ 9 Haddington Place EH7 4AL ☎ 0131 524 2090; www.syha.org.uk).

rooms have fridges containing fresh milk and water, and smart bathrooms. Breakfast is served at one large communal table. No smoking and no children under 15.

➕ C9 ✉ 15 Glengyle Terrace EH3 9LN ☎ 0131 228 1973 🚌 24, 41

## IVY HOUSE

www.ivyguesthouse.com

Pretty Victorian guesthouse south of the city. The eight bedrooms come in various sizes. Good substantial breakfasts.

➕ Off map ✉ 7 Mayfield Gardens EH9 2AX ☎ 0131 667 3411; fax 0131 620 1422 🚌 3, 7, 8, 29, 31, 37, 49, 37

## KEW HOUSE

www.kewhouse.com

Forming part of a listed Victorian terrace, Kew House is spotless throughout and has six bright bedrooms and a comfortable lounge offering supper and snack options. Near Murrayfield Stadium. No smoking.

➕ Off map ✉ 1 Kew Terrace, Murrayfield EH12 5JE ☎ 0131 313 0700; fax 0131 313 0747 🚌 12, 26, 31

## TRAVELODGE EDINBURGH CENTRAL

www.travelodge.co.uk

Travelodge offers 193 good-quality, good-value en suite rooms in a convenient central location. The spacious rooms make it ideal for families.

➕ F6 ✉ 33 St. Mary's Street EH1 1TAE ☎ 0870 191 1637; fax 0131 557 3681 🚌 35, 36

# Mid-Range Hotels

### PRICES

Expect to pay between £75 and £150 per night for a double room in a mid-range hotel.

## APEX CITY HOTEL

www.apexhotels.co.uk
Modern and stylish hotel set in the historic and fashionable square dominated by Edinburgh Castle above. There are 119 fresh, contemporary rooms. Drinks and meals can be taken in the Agua Bar and Restaurant, a smart open-plan area in dark wood and chrome. Use of the spa at the nearby International Hotel.
🕂 D7 ✉ 61 Grassmarket EH1 2JF ☎ 0131 243 3456; fax 0131 225 6346 🚌 2

## THE BALLANTRAE

www.ballantraehotel.co.uk
This hotel, in a listed Georgian town house in New Town, is in the lower end of the mid-range price bracket. The 34 spacious rooms feature period detail. The honeymoon suite has a four-poster bed and the family room has a Jacuzzi. Next door the Ballantrae Apartments offer self-catering in one- or two-bedroom apartments providing an independent way of visiting the city.
🕂 E4 ✉ 8 York Place EH1 3EP ☎ 0131 478 4748; fax 0131 478 4749 🚌 4, 8, 10, 11, 12, 15, 16, 17, 26, 44, 45

## BEST WESTERN EDINBURGH CITY

www.bestwesternedinburgh
city.co.uk
Occupying a site that was once a maternity hospital, this tasteful conversion is located close to central Edinburgh. The 52 spacious bedrooms are smartly modern and well equipped with fridges. There is a cozy, yet stylish, bar and restaurant.
🕂 D7 ✉ 79 Lauriston Place EH3 9HZ ☎ 0131 622 7979; fax 0131 622 7900 🚌 2

### ACCOMMODATION

Apart from the larger more obvious hotels, Edinburgh has numerous guest houses and small family-run hotels. The latter will have more rooms, normally all with en suite facilities; they will probably be licensed to serve alcohol and they will provide breakfast, dinner and sometimes lunch. For something more homelike, bed-and-breakfasts are usually very comfortable, and give you the opportunity to sample a real Scottish breakfast. (▷ 108). If you intend to stay outside the city and just go in for individual days to sight-see, it can be worth considering self-catering accommodation (▷ 111, panel). There are several holiday parks nearby that offer holiday homes and touring caravan and camping pitches for the lower budget.

## CHANNINGS

www.channings.co.uk
Friendly town house with traditional elegance, which offers country-style tranquillity in a West End setting. The 41 rooms vary in size but all are decorated with style.
🕂 Off map ✉ South Learmonth Gardens EH4 1EZ ☎ 0131 315 2226; fax 0131 322 9631 🚌 19, 37, 37A

## DALMAHOY HOTEL MARRIOTT & COUNTRY CLUB

www.marriott.co.uk
An imposing Georgian mansion in beautiful parkland, 11km (7 miles) southwest of the city. Most of the 215 spacious bedrooms have great views of the Pentland Hills. Guests have the use of two golf courses, a pool, tennis and a health and beauty club.
🕂 Off map ✉ Kirknewton EH27 8EB ☎ 0131 333 1845; fax 0131 333 1433

## DUNSTANE HOUSE

www.dunstane-hotel-edinburgh.co.uk
In the city's West End close to Haymarket station, this 1850s Victorian mansion house has retained much of its architectural grandeur, lending a country-house atmosphere. Some of the 16 bedrooms have four-poster beds.
🕂 Off map ✉ 4 West Coates, Haymarket EH12 5JQ ☎ 0131 337 6169; fax 0131 337 6060 🚌 12, 26, 31

## EXPRESS BY HOLIDAY INN

www.ichotelsgroup.com
Well positioned for New Town, Princes Street and all the shops, this hotel is opposite several theatres and the Omni Leisure Centre. The 161 rooms are clean and practical. A continental-style buffet breakfast is included.
➕ F4 ✉ Picardy Place EH1 3JT ☎ 0131 558 2300; fax 0131 558 2323 🚌 1, 4, 5, 8, 11, 12, 16, 17, 19, 25, 26, 45

## GERALD'S PLACE

www.geraldsplace.com
Delightfully located opposite 200-year-old private gardens, this luxury bed-and-breakfast in a Georgian terrace has just two double rooms with private bathrooms. Guests will be given Gerald's personal attention to ensure a perfect stay. Delicious Scottish breakfast included.
➕ D4 ✉ 21b Abercromby Place EH3 6QE ☎ 0131 558 7017 🚌 8, 10, 11, 12, 16

## HOLYROOD HOTEL

www.macdonaldhotels.co.uk
This impressive business hotel, next to the new Scottish Parliament Building, offers extensive facilities, including conference suites and a spa. There are 156 rooms.
➕ G6 ✉ Holyrood Road EH8 6AE ☎ 0870 194 2106; fax 0131 550 4545 🚌 35

## JURY'S INN

www.jurysdoyle.com
A modern hotel in the heart of the city, close to Waverley Station and the Royal Mile. The 186 bedrooms are bright and airy. There is a pub and informal restaurant, which also serves a canteen-style breakfast (not included in the room price).
➕ F6 ✉ 43 Jeffrey Street EH1 1DH ☎ 0131 200 3300; fax 0131 200 0400 🚌 36

## KILDONAN LODGE

www.kildonanlodgehotel.co.uk
Small hotel with 12 beautifully restored bedrooms—some with spas and four-posters—in an elegant Victorian house, where nothing is too much trouble. Pre-dinner drinks can be taken in the lounge in front of an open fire.
➕ Off map ✉ 27

Craigmillar Park EH16 5PE ☎ 0131 667 2793; fax 0131 667 9777 🚌 3, 7, 8, 29, 37, 47, 49

## MELVILLE CASTLE

www.melvillecastle.com
If you want to stay outside the city, try this castellated mansion set in 20ha (50 acres) of wooded grounds 13km (8 miles) to the south. Impressively refurbished and complemented by good meals served in the vaulted cellar bar and brasserie.
➕ Off map ✉ Melville Gate EH18 1AP ☎ 0131 654 0088; fax 0131 654 4666 🚌 3

## LE MONDE

www.lemondehotel.com
This should really be in the expensive range, but you can just squeeze the club-class room rate into this mid-range category and this stylish boutique hotel does do some good out-of-season deals. All 18 rooms are themed on cities from around the globe. Also bar, brasserie and basement nightclub.
➕ D5 ✉ 16 George Street EH2 2PF ☎ 0131 270 3900; fax 0131 270 3901 🚌 13, 19, 37, 41

## POINT HOTEL

www.point-hotel.co.uk
A distinctive structure shadowed by the castle, this 140-room hotel blends elegance with minimalist design.
➕ B7 ✉ 34 Bread Street EH3 9AF ☎ 0131 221 5555; fax 0131 221 9929 🚌 2

# Luxury Hotels

## PRICES

Expect to pay over £150 per night for a double room for a luxury hotel.

## BALMORAL

www.thebalmoralhotel.com
An impressive landmark in the heart of the city. After a major facelift, the 188 bedrooms now have a contemporary feel, while retaining the Balmoral's grandeur.
🔳 E5 ✉ 1 Princes Street EH2 2EQ ☎ 0131 556 2414; fax 0131 557 3747 🚌 3, 10, 17, 23, 24, 27, 44 and others

## THE BONHAM

www.thebonham.com
A West End hotel that offers modern public rooms with mood lighting and striking art, and 48 bedrooms combining high standards of style with 21st-century technology. There is a refreshing contemporary feel throughout. Imaginative dinners highlight the chef's commitment and good use of local fresh produce (▷ 106).
🔳 A6 ✉ 35 Drumsheugh Gardens EH3 7RN ☎ 0131 226 6050; fax 0131 226 6080 🚌 13

## BRUNTSFIELD HOTEL

www.thebruntsfield.co.uk
Overlooking Bruntsfield Links, this chic hotel has stylish lounge areas and 71 bedrooms varying in size. Meals are served in a conservatory-style restaurant.
🔳 B9 ✉ 69–74 Bruntsfield Place EH10 4HH ☎ 0131 229 1393; fax 0131 229 5634 🚌 11, 15, 16, 17, 23

## GLASSHOUSE

www.theetoncollection.com
Modern glass architecture embraces a striking church façade as you enter this chic boutique hotel. The 65 rooms have floor-to-ceiling windows that ensure spectacular views over Calton Hill. Rooftop bar and garden.
🔳 F4 ✉ 2 Greenside Place EH1 3AA ☎ 0131 525 8200; fax 0131 525 8205 🚌 4, 7, 10, 11, 12, 16, 22, 34

## THE HOWARD

www.thehoward.com
Three Georgian houses

## PEACE AND QUIET

After spending a few days exploring Edinburgh's environs, you may be tempted to take to the countryside for some peace and quiet. Dalhousie Castle and Spa (✉ Bonnyrigg EH19 3JB ☎ 01875 820153; fax 0131 01875 821936; www.dalhousiecastle.co.uk) can provide just that, plus luxurious pampering. This magnificent 13th-century castle, amid manicured lawns and parkland, is about 11km (7 miles) outside Edinburgh. The 36 theme rooms are named after historical figures and are opulently decorated. Facilities include two restaurants, and a sauna and spa.

make up this sophisticated hotel, a short walk from Princes Street. The 18 good-size rooms have bathrooms with claw-foot baths, and the elegant day rooms are decked out with chandeliers, lavish drapes and murals.
🔳 C3 ✉ 34 Great King Street EH3 6QH ☎ 0131 557 3500; fax 0131 557 6515 🚌 13

## MALMAISON

www.malmaison.com
Stylish hotel with 100 bedrooms; some in bold stripes, others in subtle tones; some have views of the port at Leith.
🔳 Off map ✉ 1 Tower Place, Leith EH6 7DB ☎ 0131 468 5000; fax 0131 468 5002 🚌 16, 22, 35, 36

## THE SCOTSMAN

www.thescotsmanhotel.co.uk
Once head office to *The Scotsman* newspaper in the Old Town, but now transformed into a state-of-the-art hotel, where classic elegance blends with high-tech design. The 69 rooms are in various sizes and styles. The galleried North Bridge Brasserie restaurant offers an informal and flexible dining option or dine in style in the Vermilion restaurant (▷ 44). The dimly lit subterranean Escape leisure club boasts an unusual stainless steel swimming pool.
🔳 E5 ✉ 20 North Bridge EH1 1YT ☎ 0131 556 5565; fax 0131 652 3652 🚌 3, 5, 7, 30, 31, 33, 37

Edinburgh is compact and easy to navigate by foot. However, city buses are frequent and an efficient way of getting around, especially to outlying areas. The Essential Facts give inside knowledge of the city.

Need to Know

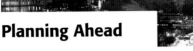

# Planning Ahead

## When to Go

Edinburgh lies on the eastern side of Scotland, which is cooler, windier and drier than the west. At any time of year you are likely to meet rain, but the chances are it will not last for long. Many tourist sights close in winter, but major city museums stay open year-round.

**TIME**

GMT (Greenwich Mean Time) is standard. BST (British Summer Time) is 1 hour ahead (late Mar–late Oct).

| AVERAGE DAILY MAXIMUM TEMPERATURES | | | | | | | | | | | |
|---|---|---|---|---|---|---|---|---|---|---|---|
| JAN | FEB | MAR | APR | MAY | JUN | JUL | AUG | SEP | OCT | NOV | DEC |
| 39°F | 39°F | 43°F | 48°F | 54°F | 61°F | 63°F | 61°F | 59°F | 54°F | 45°F | 41°F |
| 4°C | 4°C | 6°C | 9°C | 12°C | 16°C | 17°C | 16°C | 15°C | 12°C | 7°C | 5°C |

**Spring** (March to May) has the best chance of clear skies and sunny days.

**Summer** (June to August) is unpredictable–it may be hot and sunny, but it can also be cloudy and wet. This is the time you can get *haar* (sea mist) that shrouds the city in thick mist, although this can happen at other times of the year as well.

**Autumn** (September to November) is usually more settled and there's a good chance of fine weather, but nothing is guaranteed.

**Winter** (December to February) can be cold, dark, wet and dreary, but there are also sparkling, clear, sunny days of frost, when the light is brilliant.

## WHAT'S ON

**January** *Burns Night* (25 Jan): the birthday of the city's national poet, celebrated throughout with haggis and whisky.

**April** *Edinburgh Science Festival*: science and technology events at various venues.

*Easter Festival*: Over 4,000 people gather in the city on Easter Sunday to celebrate cultural diversity, youth, happiness and heritage.

*Ceilidh Culture*: events centred around traditional Scottish arts.

**May** *Scottish International Children's Festival*: Britain's largest performing arts festival for young people.

**June** *Royal Highland Show*: Scotland's biggest agricultural show.

*Edinburgh Marathon.*

**July/August** *Edinburgh International Jazz & Blues Festival*: 10 days of jazz performed by big names and new talent.

**August** *Edinburgh International Festival*: over three weeks, some of the world's best plays, opera, music and dance.

*Edinburgh Festival Fringe*: A chance for the amateurs to join the professionals.

*Edinburgh Military Tattoo*: (▷ 5).

*Edinburgh International Film Festival*: (▷ 41).

*International Book Festival*: occupies a tented village in Charlotte Square.

**September** *Mela*: a vibrant celebration of cultural diversity with music, dance and street performers.

**November/December** *Capital Christmas*: German street market and more.

**December/January** *Edinburgh Hogmanay*: (▷ 13).

## Useful Websites

### www.edinburgh.org
Edinburgh's official website for tourists has up-to-date, comprehensive information on city attractions, events, guided tours, shopping, accommodation, eating out and lots more.

### www.visitscotland.com
The official Scotland Tourist Board website, with a comprehensive database of information covering everything from weather, transport and events to shopping, nightlife and accommodation throughout Scotland.

### www.eif.co.uk
A comprehensive guide to What's On at the Edinburgh International Festival. There is also the chance to join the mailing list.

### www.edinburghguide.com
An informative guide to attractions, entertainment, recreation, eating out and accommodation, plus links to other sites.

### www.nms.ac.uk
The National Museum of Scotland looks after many of Scotland's important museum collections. Its website provides detailed information about the museums in its care.

### www.undiscoveredscotland.co.uk
An online guide to Scotland. The Edinburgh section has many useful links to other good sources of information.

### www.nts.org.uk
The National Trust for Scotland looks after historic buildings in Scotland, including some in Edinburgh. Its website gives updated information about all the properties it is responsible for.

### www.historic-scotland.gov.uk
The website has information on more than 300 listed buildings and ancient sites safeguarded by Historic Scotland.

## PRIME TRAVEL SITES

**www.fodors.com**
A complete travel-planning site. You can research prices and weather; reserve air tickets, cars and rooms; pose questions (and get answers) to fellow visitors; and find links to other sites.

**www.theAA.com**
Find out more about the wide range of travel publications and services the AA has to offer; click on hotels and B&B to find accommodation, or pubs and restaurants for eating and drinking options.

## INTERNET CAFÉS

**easyInternetcafé**
🔲 C5 ✉ 58 Rose Street EH2 2YQ ☎ 0131 220 3577
🕐 Daily 7.30am–10pm
💷 £1 per 30 minutes

**Moviebank**
🔲 E3 ✉ 53 London Street EH3 6LX ☎ 0131 557 1011
🕐 Mon–Sat 2–10, Sun 2–9
💷 3p per minute
(no minimum)

# Getting There

## ENTRY REQUIREMENTS

For the latest passport and visa information, look up the British embassy website at www.britishembassy.ie or the United States embassy at www.usembassy.ie or call or write to the office (▷ 117).

## CUSTOMS

● EU nationals do not have to declare goods imported for their own use, although you may be questioned by customs officials if you have large amounts of certain items.

● The limits for non-EU visitors are 200 cigarettes or 50 cigars or 250g of tobacco; 1 litre of alcohol (over 22 per cent alcohol) or 2 litres of wine; 50g of perfume.

## AIRPORTS

There are direct flights to Edinburgh's international airport from other parts of the UK and from continental Europe, but most transatlantic flights are routed via London.

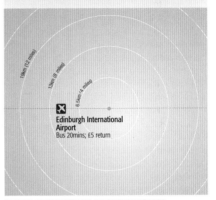

19km (12 miles)

13km (8 miles)

6.5km (4 miles)

Edinburgh International Airport
Bus 20mins; £5 return

### FROM EDINBURGH INTERNATIONAL AIRPORT

Edinburgh's airport (☎ 0870 040 0007; www. baa.com) is located at Ingliston, 10km (6 miles) west of the city, off the A8.

Airlink operates a coach service to the heart of Edinburgh every 10 minutes on weekdays, less often at weekends and in the evening. The journey takes about 25 minutes and costs £5 return, £3 one-way. Tickets can be bought from Tourist Information inside the airport, from the ticket booth or on the bus. A map showing the route is available from the information desk and there is a map inside the bus. The route brings you in past the zoo and Murrayfield sports stadium, and goes all the way along Princes Street to Waverley Bridge and the rail station. Buses leave from the arrivals area in front of the terminal building.

Taxis wait outside the arrivals hall in the rank beside the coach park. The journey takes about 25 minutes and costs around £15.

Edinburgh Airport has a reasonable range of facilities, including a tourist information desk, a few shops, bureaux de change, restaurants, car-rental firms and a left-luggage office.

## INTERNAL FLIGHTS

You can get to the following places directly from Edinburgh International Airport: Aberdeen, Inverness, Kirkwall, Sumburgh and Wick; also to Birmingham, Bournemouth, Bristol, East Midlands, Guernsey, Humberside, Jersey, London Heathrow, London Gatwick, London Stansted, Manchester, Norwich and Southampton.

## ARRIVING BY RAIL

Edinburgh has two major rail stations: Edinburgh Haymarket and Edinburgh Waverley. Waverley is a main hub for travel within Scotland, and is well served with tourist information desks and other facilities. The main rail companies operating from England to Edinburgh are Virgin and GNER and most internal services are run by First ScotRail (www.firstgroup.com/scotland). For further details of fares and services contact the National Rail Enquiry Service (☎ 08457 484950; www.nationalrail.co.uk).

## ARRIVING BY COACH

Coaches arrive in Edinburgh from England, Wales and all over Scotland at the St. Andrews Street bus station. The main coach companies operating to and from here are National Express (☎ 08705 808080; www.national express.com) and Scottish Citylink (☎ 08705 505050; www.citylink.co.uk).

## ARRIVING BY CAR

One-way systems, narrow streets, 'red' routes and dedicated bus routes make driving in the city difficult. Limited on-street parking is mostly pay-and-display 8.30am–6.30pm Mon–Sat. There are designated parking areas, to the south of Princes Street; the biggest is at Greenside Place, off Leith Street. Petrol stations are normally open Mon–Sat 6am–10pm, Sun 8am–8pm, though some (often self-service) are open 24 hours. All take credit cards and many have well stocked shops.

### INSURANCE

Check your insurance coverage and buy a supplementary policy if needed. EU nationals receive reduced-cost medical treatment with an EHIC card. Obtain this card before leaving home. Full health and travel insurance is still advised.

### CONSULATES

All embassies are located in London but the following consulates are based in Edinburgh:
● French Consulate ✉ 21 Randolph Crescent EH3 7TT ☎ 0131 225 7954
● German Consulate ✉ 16 Eglinton Crescent EH12 5DG ☎ 0131 337 2323
● Netherlands Consulate ✉ Thistle Court, 1–2 Thistle Street EH2 1DD ☎ 0131 220 3226
● Spanish Consulate ✉ 63 North Castle Street EH2 3LJ ☎ 0131 220 1843
● US Consulate ✉ 3 Regent Terrace EH7 5BW ☎ 0131 556 8315

# Getting Around

● The official source of information for tourists is www.edinburgh.org and VisitScotland, which has a very useful website www.visitscotland.com and National Booking and Information service ☎ 0845 22 55 121.

● Edinburgh and Scotland Information Centre ✉ 3 Princes Street, EH2 2QP ☎ 0845 22 55 121 🕐 May, Jun, Sep Mon–Sat 9–7, Sun 10–7; Jul, Aug Mon–Sat 9–8, Sun 10–8; Apr, Oct Mon–Sat 9–6, Sun 10–6; Nov–end Mar Mon–Sat 9–5, Sun 10–5

● Edinburgh Airport Tourist Information Desk ✉ Ingliston EH12 9DN 🕐 Apr–end Oct Mon–Sat 6.30am–10.30pm; Nov–end Mar daily 7am–9pm

**LOST PROPERTY**

● Property found and handed to the police is sent to Police Headquarters ✉ Fettes Avenue ☎ 0131 311 3131 🕐 Mon–Fri 9–5

● There are lost property departments at Edinburgh Airport ☎ 0131 344 3486; Waverley train station ☎ 0131 550 2333; and Lothian buses ✉ Annandale Street, off Leith Walk ☎ 0131 558 8858 🕐 Mon–Fri 10–1.30

● Report losses of passports to the police.

## BY BUS

Lothian Buses (☎ 0131 555 6363; www.lothianbuses.co.uk) is the main bus company operating throughout the city (the buses are either maroon and white or red and white). Bus stops display the name of the stop and the bus numbers for regular and night services. Pay on boarding and ensure you have the exact fare, as no change is given. Put the money into the slot in front of the driver, then take your ticket from the machine behind the driver. The standard adult fare for a single journey is £1. A flat-rate single journey at night (any distance) is £2. A CitySingle costs £20 for 21 trips (meaning there is no need to worry about having the right change) and is available from Lothian Travel Shops (▷ below). A child (5–15) pays 60p to travel any distance. You can buy a Dayticket from the driver for a day's unlimited travel (adult £2.30, child £2).

## TICKETS

Timetables and tickets are available at the Travel Shops (✉ 27 Hanover Street; Shandwick Place; Waverley Bridge 🕐 Mon–Sat 8.15–6, Sun 9.30–5—Waverley Bridge only). An enlarged map and timetable on the bridge outside Waverley Station has additional information about the night bus service into the suburbs.

## TAXIS

Licensed taxis operate a reliable service day and night; fares are metered and strictly regulated. Cabs can be found at designated ranks like Waverley Park or Pollock, can be hailed along the road, or called by phone (City Cabs ☎ 0131 228 1211; Computer Cabs ☎ 0131 228 2555).

## CAR RENTAL

Major rental firms such as Avis, Hertz and Budget have offices at Edinburgh Airport ☎ 0870 040 0007. There are also local firms, including Arnold Clark ☎ 0845 607 4500 and Edinburgh Self Drive ☎ 0131 229 8686.

## EDINBURGH PASS

Launched in spring 2005, this card gives free access to more than 25 attractions in Edinburgh and the Lothians. It also includes free bus travel, including airport bus transfer, and offers from some shops, restaurants and Festival events. A free guidebook explains what's on offer. Cost: 1-day pass £20, 2-day £36 and 3-day £45. You can buy online at www.edinburgh.org/pass or purchase from the Tourist Information Centres at the airport or in the city.

## ORGANIZED SIGHTSEEING

A guided tour is a good way to gain more in-depth knowledge about Edinburgh. If time is short, take one of the open-top buses that wind their way around the city sights; all tours depart from Waverley Bridge and there are four types to choose from, including one where you can hop on and hop off at your leisure (☎ 0131 220 0770; www.edinburghtour.com). Various companies offer coach tours in and around the city. Try Rabbie's Trail Burners (☎ 0131 226 3133; www.rabbies.com), who run mini-coach (16 seater) tours to destinations such as Loch Ness and St. Andrews. For those who prefer two wheels, another option is Adrian's Edinburgh City Cycle Tour (☎ 07966 447 206), a three-hour tour starting from Holyrood Palace gates, with all equipment supplied.

## WALKING TOURS

Mercat Walking Tours:
Walks where you can explore secret underground vaults, ghost walks and fascinating history tours with dramatic commentaries.
✉ Mercat House, 28 Blair Street EH1 1QR
☎ 0131 557 6464; www.mercattours.com

The Cadies and Witchery Tours:
Light-hearted ghostly tours through the darker parts of Old Edinburgh.
✉ 84 West Bow  ☎ 0131 225 6745;
www.witcherytours.com

### VISITORS WITH DISABILITIES

● Capability Scotland (✉ 11 Ellersly Road, Edinburgh EH12 6HY ☎ 0131 313 5510; www.capability-scotland.org.uk) can advise on travel requirements to ensure a less stressful trip.
● www.disabledgo.info is an internet service giving information to people with disabilities to research access and find other useful advice when visiting Edinburgh. Restaurants, cafés, shops and attractions are all covered.
● A wide range of information for visitors with disabilities can be found in VisitScotland's publication Practical Information for Visitors with Disabilities, available from the tourist board or from tourist offices.

### STUDENT VISITORS

● Students can get reduced-cost entry to some museums and attractions by showing a valid student card. There is some good budget accommodation available.
● There are reduced fares on buses and trains for under 16s.

# Essential Facts

## MONEY/CREDIT CARDS

● Credit cards are widely accepted.
● ATMs are readily available.

## MONEY

Scotland's currency is pounds sterling (£), in notes of £5, £10, £20, £50 and £100. Coins are issued in values of 1p, 2p, 5p, 10p, 20p, 50p, £1 and £2. England's notes are legal tender in Scotland.

£5

£10

£50

## TIPPING

It is customary to tip the following:
● Restaurants (where service is not included) 10–15 per cent
● Tour guides £1–£2
● Taxis 10 per cent
● Hairdressers 10 per cent
● Chambermaids 50p–£1 per day
● Porters 50p–£1 per bag

## ELECTRICITY

● Britain is on 240 volts AC, and plugs have three square pins. If you are bringing an electrical appliance from another country where the voltage is the same, a plug adaptor will suffice. If the voltage is different, as in the US—110 volts—you need a converter.
● Small appliances such as razors can run on a 50-watt converter, while heating appliances, irons and hairdryers require a 1,600-watt converter.

## EMERGENCY TELEPHONE NUMBERS

● Police, Ambulance, Fire ☎ 999 or 112.
● For non-emergency police enquiries contact the nearest police station (see Directory Enquiries, panel, ▷ 122).
● If you break down driving your own car you can call the Automobile Association and join on the spot if you are not already a member (☎ 0800 887766). Check if your home country membership entitles you to reciprocal assistance. If you are driving a rental car, call the emergency number in your documentation.

## MEDICINES AND MEDICAL TREATMENT

● Citizens from the EU are entitled to free or reduced-cost NHS (National Health Service) treatment—bring the EHIC card from your home country. Full health and travel insurance is still advised. Those visiting from outside the EU should have full travel and health insurance.
● For medical emergencies ☎ 999 or 112 or go to the nearest hospital casualty department (emergency room). The 24-hour casualty department is at the Royal Infirmary of Edinburgh ⊠ 51 Little France Crescent, Old Dalkeith Road EH16 4SA ☎ 0131 536 1000. For minor injuries the Western General Hospital (⊠ Crewe Road South EH4 2XU ☎ 0131 537 1000) has a walk-in service ◑ Daily 8–9. No appointment is necessary. Telephone advice is also available from the unit if you are in doubt or need to talk to someone. The unit is staffed by specialist nurse practitioners who can assess, diagnose

and treat and/or refer people for further treatment if required.

● Eye injuries: there is an emergency department at the Princess Alexandra Eye Pavilion ✉ Chalmers Street ☎ 0131 536 3753/4 🕓 Mon–Fri 8.30–5. Go to the A&E at the Royal Infirmary outside these hours.

● To find the nearest doctor, dentist or pharmacy ask at your hotel or call the Primary Care Centre ☎ 0131 537 8488 for general enquiries. For further details of dentists contact ☎ 0131 537 8424.

● Pharmacies and large supermarkets have a range of medicines available over the counter but items such as antibiotics require a doctor's prescription.

● There are no 24-hour pharmacies in Edinburgh. Boots the Chemist (✉ 48 Shandwick Place ☎ 0131 225 6757) has the longest opening hours 🕓 Mon–Fri 8am–9pm, Sat 8am–7pm, Sun 10am–5pm.

## NATIONAL HOLIDAYS
● New Year's Day (1 January)
● New Year's Holiday (2 January)
● Good Friday
● Easter Monday
● First Monday in May
● Last Monday in May
● First Monday in August
● Last Monday in August
● Christmas Day (25 December)
● Boxing Day (26 December)
● Most places of interest close on New Year's Day, 1 May and Christmas, while others close on all public holidays.

## OPENING TIMES
● Banks: Mon–Fri 9.30–4.30; larger branches may open Sat morning.
● Post offices: Mon–Fri 9–5.30, Sat 9–12.
● Shops: Mon–Sat 9–5 or 5.30. Newsagents and some shops may open on Sun.
● Museums: opening times vary widely, see individual entries.

### SENSIBLE PRECAUTIONS
● Levels of violent crime are relatively low but there are areas to avoid, as in every city. Places to avoid at night include the backstreet and dockside areas of Leith, *wynds* (narrow lanes) off the Royal Mile, the footpaths across the Meadows and other unlit urban areas.
● Scottish police officers wear a peaked flat hat with black-and-white check band and are friendly and approachable.
● Petty theft is the most common problem, so don't carry more cash than you need and beware of pickpockets, especially in the main tourist areas and on public transport. Take care of bags and do not leave them on backs of chairs.

### TOILETS
● Generally these are well-located, plentiful and free in built-up areas. There may be a small charge to use toilets at some rail stations.
● It is not acceptable for those who are not customers to use the toilets in pubs, cafés and restaurants. Buy a drink first.

## NEWSPAPERS AND MAGAZINES

● *The Scotsman* is at the quality end of the market.
● Scotland's popular tabloid daily newspaper is the *Daily Record*.
● *The Sunday Post* is a top-selling institution.
● *Scotland on Sunday* is a heavyweight that vies with the *Sunday Herald* for the more serious readership.
● *The List* is a lively fortnightly listings magazine, giving excellent coverage for Edinburgh.
● Newspapers from around the world, including foreign-language papers, can be purchased at airports, larger train stations and some newspaper shops.

## TELEPHONE SERVICES

● Various companies offer Directory Enquiries services. The British Telecom numbers are:
● Directory Enquiries ☎ 118 500
● International Directory Enquiries ☎ 118 505
● International Operator ☎ 155
● Operator ☎ 100

## POST OFFICES

● Main post office ✉ St. James Centre, St. Andrew Square ☎ 0845 722 3344
🕑 Mon–Sat 9–5.30. Most other post offices open 9–12 on Sat.
● Many newspaper shops and supermarkets sell stamps.
● Postboxes are painted red; collection times are shown on each box.

## RADIO AND TELEVISION

● Scotland is served by the UK's national radio stations (BBC), and has some of its own for more Scottish coverage.
● BBC Radio Scotland has a loyal following; it broadcasts a broad mix of news, discussion, travel, music shows and weather forecasts.
● There are also several local radio stations for news bulletins, and commercial stations including Radio Forth (serving Edinburgh).
● There are five main national terrestrial TV channels in Britain. Scotland's mainstream television choice is essentially what is broadcast from south of the border, with local interest, home-based material slotted in.

## TELEPHONES

● The code for Edinburgh is 0131. There is a full list of area codes and country codes in all phone books. Omit the area code when making a local call.
● Phone cards for payphones can be used in units of £2, £5 and £10. Coins of 10p, 20p, 50p and £1 are also accepted. Credit and debit cards can be used to make calls from many BT (British Telecom) payphones (50p minimum charge; 20p per minute for all inland calls). Payphones in hotels and pubs can be very expensive as the venues set their own profit margin.
● Cheap rate is after 6pm weekdays and all day Saturday and Sunday.
● To call the US from Scotland dial 00 1, followed by the number.
● To call Scotland from the US, dial 011 44, then omit the 0 from the area code.

# Language

Standard English is the official language of Scotland, and spoken everywhere. However, like other corners of Britain, the Scottish people have their own variations on the language and the way it is spoken. You should have no difficulty understanding the people of Edinburgh, who tend automatically to moderate their accent when speaking to non-Scots. But many Scottish words and phrases are used in everyday conversation.

## COMMON WORDS AND PHRASES

| | |
|---|---|
| *auld* | old |
| *awfy* | very |
| *aye/naw* | yes/no |
| *belong* | come from |
| *ben* | hill, mountain |
| *birle* | spin, turn |
| *blether* | to chatter, gossip |
| *bonnie* | pretty, attractive |
| *braw* | fine, good |
| *burn* | stream |
| *canny* | cunnning, clever |
| *ceilidh* | party or dance |
| *couthy* | comfortable |
| *douce* | gentle and kind |
| *dram* | a measure of whisky |
| *een* | eyes |
| *fash* | bother |
| *gae* | go |
| *gloaming* | dusk |
| *guttered* | drunk |
| *haar* | sea mist |
| *Hogmanay* | New Year's Eve |
| *ken* | to know |
| *kirk* | church |
| *lassie* | girl |
| *lum* | chimney |
| *messages* | shopping |
| *nicht* | night |
| *och* | oh |
| *Sassenach* | non-Scottish person |
| *stay* | live |
| *trews* | tartan trousers |
| *wee* | small |

# Timeline

## EARLY SETTLERS

The area was first settled by hunting tribes around 3000BC and in about 1000BC the first farmers were joined by immigrant Beaker People, who introduced pottery and metalworking skills. Parts of Scotland were held by the Romans for a short time and after their departure in the 5th century AD the area suffered waves of invasion.

## THE MACALPINS

Northumbrians held southern Scotland for 33 years, but were defeated in 1018 by MacAlpin king Malcolm II. Malcolm III married Margaret, sister of Edgar Atheling, heir to the English throne, but was usurped by William the Conqueror.

*From left to right: Robert the Bruce statue; James VI of Scotland; the Forth Rail Bridge; posters for the Edinburgh Festival; Holyrood Park hosts Fringe Festival events*

*1314* Thomas Randolph retakes Edinburgh Castle from the English on behalf of Robert the Bruce.

*1329* Edinburgh receives Royal Charter from Robert the Bruce.

*1349* Thirty per cent of Edinburgh's population is killed by the Black Death.

*1513* James IV is killed at the Battle of Flodden; work begins on Flodden Wall for the defence of Edinburgh.

*1544* Edinburgh is attacked by English forces, who fail to take the city.

*1566* Holyroodhouse is the scene of Darnley's grizzly murder of David Rizzio, the darling of Mary, Queen of Scots.

*1603* James VI moves his Court to London after acceding to the English throne.

*1633* Edinburgh officially becomes capital city of Scotland.

*1639* Parliament House is built and used by the Scottish Parliament until 1707.

*1692–8* A run of bad harvests leads to riots.

*1702–7* The Scottish Parliament debates and finally ratifies the Act of Union, voting itself out of existence.

**1736** The Porteous Riots.

**1767** First plans for New Town adopted.

**1817** *The Scotsman* is first printed.

**1824** The world's first municipal fire service is founded after fire rages in the High Street.

**1890** Forth Rail Bridge opens.

**1895** Electric street lighting is introduced.

**1947** The first Edinburgh International Festival.

**1970** Commonwealth Pool and Meadowbank Stadium are built for the 1970 Commonwealth Games.

**1971** St. James Centre opens and further demolition of Georgian houses in Princes Street takes place.

**1986** The Commonwealth Games are held in Edinburgh for a second time.

**1999** The Scottish Parliament sits for the first time since 1707.

**2004** The Queen opens the striking new Parliament building.

**2007** New transport strategy to be developed, bringing trams to the city by 2111.

### EDINBURGH'S FAMOUS

Some of Edinburgh's most famous sons have had a significant impact on our lives. Alexander Graham Bell invented the telephone in 1847, and anaesthetics were pioneered by James Young Simpson. John Knox reformed Scotland's religion and architect Robert Adam and artists Henry Raeburn and Allan Ramsay brought their flair to the buildings of the city. The literary impact has been phenomenal, through the romances of Sir Walter Scott, who was born in the city in 1771, and the detective stories of Sir Arthur Conan Doyle. More fame comes from Robert Louis Stevenson, author of *Kidnapped* and *Treasure Island*, who was born here in 1850, and actor Sean Connery, who spent his early days here.

**NEED TO KNOW** TIMELINE

125

# Index

# CITYPACK TOP 25
# Edinburgh

**WRITTEN BY** Hilary Weston and Jackie Staddon
**ADDITIONAL WRITING** Sally Roy
**DESIGN CONCEPT** Kate Harling
**COVER DESIGN AND DESIGN WORK** Jacqueline Bailey
**INDEXER** Marie Lorimer
**IMAGE RETOUCHING AND REPRO** Michael Moody, Sarah Montgomery and Matt Swann
**EDITORIAL MANAGEMENT** Apostrophe S Limited
**SERIES EDITOR** Paul Mitchell

© **AUTOMOBILE ASSOCIATION DEVELOPMENTS LIMITED 2008**
First published 2006
Colour separation by Keenes
Printed and bound by Leo, China

A CIP catalogue record for this book is available from the British Library.

**ISBN 978-0-7495-5489-7**

Published by AA Publishing, a trading name of Automobile Association Developments Limited, whose registered office is Fanum House, Basing View, Basingstoke, Hampshire RG21 4EA. Registered number 1878835.

A03144

This product includes mapping data licensed from Ordnance Survey® with the permission of the Controller of Her Majesty's Stationery Office. © Crown copyright 2007. All rights reserved. Licence number 100021153.
Transport map © Communicarta Ltd, UK

The Automobile Association wishes to thank the following photographers, companies and picture libraries for their assistance in the preparation of this book.

Abbreviations for the picture credits are as follows – (t) top; (b) bottom; (l) left; (r) right; (c) centre; (AA) AA World Travel Library.

**Front cover** AA/J Smith; **back cover (i)** AA/D Corrance; **(ii)** AA/C Sawyer; **(iii)** AA/J Smith; **(iv)** AA/K Paterson; **1** Edinburgh Inspiring Capital; **2–8t** AA/E Ellington; **4tl** AA/J Freeman; **5** Edinburgh Inspiring Capital; **6cl** AA/K Paterson; **6c** AA/M Taylor; **6cr** AA/J Smith; **6bl** AA/J Smith; **6bcl** AA/J Smith; **6bc** AA/J Smith; **6br** Edinburgh Inspiring Capital; **7tl** AA/J Smith; **7tc** AA/K Paterson; **7tr** Edinburgh Inspiring Capital; **7cl** AA/K Paterson; **7c** AA/K Paterson; **7cr** Edinburgh Inspiring Capital; **10ctr** Edinburgh Inspiring Capital; **10cr** Edinburgh Inspiring Capital; **10/11c** Edinburgh Inspiring Capital; **10/11b** Edinburgh Inspiring Capital; **11ctl** AA/S Whitehorne; **11cl** Edinburgh Inspiring Capital; **12br** AA/J Smith; **13(i)** AA; **13(ii)** Edinburgh Inspiring Capital; **13(iii)** Edinburgh Inspiring Capital; **13(iv)** Edinburgh Inspiring Capital; **13(v)** Edinburgh Inspiring Capital; **14tr** AA/K Paterson; **14tcr** AA/K Paterson; **14cr** AA/K Paterson; **14br** AA/IL; **15b** AA/R Elliot; **16tr** AA/K Paterson; **16cr** AA/K Paterson; **16br** Photodisc; **17tl** AA/K Paterson; **17tcl** Edinburgh Inspiring Capital; **17cl** Edinburgh Inspiring Capital; **17bl** Edinburgh Inspiring Capital; **18tr** Edinburgh Inspiring Capital; **18tcr** Edinburgh Inspiring Capital; **18cr** Edinburgh Inspiring Capital; **18br** BrandX Pics; **19(i)** Edinburgh Inspiring Capital; **19(ii)** Adam Elder/Scottish Parliament; **19(iii)** AA/K Paterson; **19(iv)** Edinburgh Inspiring Capital; **20/21** Edinburgh Inspiring Capital; **24l** AA/J Smith; **24r** AA/J Smith; **24/25** AA/J Smith; **25t** Edinburgh Inspiring Capital; **25c** AA/J Smith; **25cr** AA/J Smith; **26l** AA/D Corrance; **26c** AA/K Paterson; **26r** AA/K Paterson; **27l** Edinburgh Inspiring Capital; **27c** AA/K Paterson; **27r** Edinburgh Inspiring Capital; **28tl** AA/S Whitehorne; **28tr** AA/S Whitehorne; **28cl** AA/K Paterson; **28cr** AA/J Smith; **29t** AA/J Smith; **29cl** AA/K Paterson; **29cr** AA/K Paterson; **30l** AA/J Smith; **30r** AA/J Smith; **31l** AA/K Paterson; **31r** AA; **32–35l** AA/J Smith; **32bl** AA/J Smith; **32br** AA/S Whitehorne; **33bl** AA/J Smith; **33br** AA/K Paterson; **34bl** © The Trustees of the National Museums of Scotland; **34br** The Real Mary King's Close; **35bl** AA/S Whitehorne; **35br** AA/K Paterson; **36** AA/K Paterson; **37** AA/S Whitehorne; **38–39t** Edinburgh Inspiring Capital; **40–41t** AA/J Smith; **42–44** Edinburgh Inspiring Capital; **45** Adam Elder/Scottish Parliament; **48t** AA/J Smith; **48c** AA/K Paterson; **49t** AA/K Paterson; **49cl** AA/J Smith; **49cr** Edinburgh Inspiring Capital; **50** AA/J Smith; **50/51t** Douglas Robertson; **50/51c** AA/J Smith; **51t** Douglas Robertson; **51c** Douglas Robertson; **51cr** Douglas Robertson; **52l** AA/J Smith; **52r** AA/K Paterson; **53l** AA/K Paterson; **53c** AA/D Corrance; **53r** AA/K Paterson; **54** AA/K Paterson; **54/55** AA/K Paterson; **55t** AA; **55c** AA/J Smith; **55cr** AA/K Paterson; **56l** Our Dynamic Earth; **56r** Our Dynamic Earth; **57l** Edinburgh Inspiring Capital; **57r** Adam Elder/Scottish Parliament; **58l** AA/D Corrance; **58r** AA/J Smith; **58/59** AA/R Elliott; **59t** AA/J Smith; **59cr** AA; **60t** AA; **60bl** AA/J Smith; **60br** AA/J Smith; **61t** Adam Elder/Scottish Parliament; **62** Edinburgh Inspiring Capital; **63** AA/K Paterson; **64t** Edinburgh Inspiring Capital; **64c** AA/K Paterson; **65** AA/J Smith; **68l** AA/R Elliott; **68r** AA/K Paterson; **69l** AA/K Paterson; **69r** AA/K Paterson; **70** National Gallery of Scotland, Purchased with the aid of the Heritage Lottery Fund, The Art Fund, the Scottish Executive, the Bank of Scotland, the Royal Bank of Scotland, Sir Tom Farmer, the Dunard Fund, Mr and Mrs Kenneth Woodcock (donation made through the American Friends of the National Galleries of Scotland) and private donations 1999; **70/71t** AA/K Paterson; **70/71c** AA/K Paterson; **71t** AA/K Paterson; **71c** National Gallery of Scotland; **71cr** National Gallery of Scotland; **72** AA/I Love; **72/73t** AA/K Paterson; **72/73b** AA/K Paterson; **73** AA/K Paterson; **74l** AA/J Smith; **74r** AA/J Smith; **75–76t** AA/K Paterson; **75b** AA/K Paterson; **76bl** AA/J Smith; **76br** AA/K Paterson; **78–80t** AA/K Paterson; **81** Edinburgh Inspiring Capital; **82–83t** Edinburgh Inspiring Capital; **84–86t** AA/K Paterson; **87** AA/K Paterson; **90** AA/K Paterson; **90/91** AA/K Paterson; **92l** AA/K Paterson; **92r** AA/K Paterson; **93t** Edinburgh Inspiring Capital; **93cl** AA/D Corrance; **93cr** AA/K Paterson; **94t** AA/K Paterson; **94c** AA/K Paterson; **95t** AA/K Paterson; **95c** AA/R Elliott; **96l** AA/I Love; **96r** AA/K Paterson; **97l** AA/K Paterson; **97r** AA/K Paterson; **98l** AA/K Paterson; **98c** AA/K Paterson; **98r** Scottish National Gallery of Modern Art © Cadell Estate, courtesy of Portland Gallery, London; **99–100t** AA/K Paterson; **99bl** AA/K Paterson; **99br** AA/K Paterson; **100b** AA/K Paterson; **101t** AA/K Paterson; **101b** AA/K Paterson; **102t** AA/R Elliott; **102bl** AA/J Smith; **102br** AA/J Smith; **103** AA/J Smith; **104** AA/K Paterson; **105** AA/J Smith; **106** Imagestate; **107** AA/R Elliott; **108–112t** AA/C Sawyer; **108(i)** Edinburgh Inspiring Capital; **108 (ii)** AA; **108 (iii)** AA/D Corrance; **108 (iv)** Edinburgh Inspiring Capital; **113** Edinburgh Inspiring Capital; **114–125t** Edinburgh Inspiring Capital; **123tr** Edinburgh Inspiring Capital; **123cr** AA/J Smith; **124bl** AA/J Smith; **124bc** AA; **124br** AA/J Smith; **125bl** AA/K Paterson; **125br** AA/K Paterson

Every effort has been made to trace the copyright holders, and we apologise in advance for any accidental errors. We would be pleased to apply any corrections in any following edition of this publication.